FOUCAULT
WITH MARX

ABOUT THE AUTHOR

Jacques Bidet is a French philosopher and social theorist, currently professor emeritus in the Philosophy Department at the Université de Paris X – Nanterre. His most recent translated books are *Exploring Marx's Capital: Philosophical, Economic and Political Dimensions* (2007) and *A Critical Companion to Contemporary Marxism* (2007). He wrote the Introduction to Louis Althusser's *On The Reproduction of Capitalism* (2014).

FOUCAULT WITH MARX

JACQUES BIDET

TRANSLATED BY STEVEN CORCORAN

ZED

Zed Books

LONDON

Foucault with Marx was first published in English in 2016 by
Zed Books Ltd, The Foundry, 17 Oval Way, London SE11 5RR, UK

www.zedbooks.co.uk

Typeset in Haarlemmer by seagulls.net
Index: John Barker
Cover design: Michael Oswell

ISBN 978-1-78360-538-5 hb
ISBN 978-1-78360-537-8 pb
ISBN 978-1-78360-539-2 pdf
ISBN 978-1-78360-540-8 epub
ISBN 978-1-78360-541-5 mobi

Printed and bound by CPI Group (UK) Ltd, Croydon, CR0 4YY

To Annie, with whom I discussed this book page by page

CONTENTS

ELEMENTS OF CONCLUSION: A STRATEGY FROM BELOW

NOTE ON THE TRANSLATION

The reader will note that I have translated 'pouvoir-savoir' as 'knowledge-power', whereas it is customary to speak of 'power-knowledge' in reference to Foucault's work. This way of rendering the term seems to fit better with Jacques Bidet's thrust, however, since he aims to emphasise the power of the system of expertise theorised by Foucault, that is, not knowledge as such but the power that comes from having a certain position of competency. The rendering 'knowledge-power' also indicates that it is the other term of a bipolar dimensionality of power, the other pole being the 'property-power' theorised by Marx, from which Bidet aims at once to distinguish it while showing its varying historical relations. The agents of this knowledge-power Bidet refers to as 'competents-dirigeants', a compound noun that I have translated as 'competent-elites' in order to retain the idea of the leadership function that comes with sanctioned positions of competency (although what seems thus to get lost in the English is thereby the possibility of a tension between two terms, between competency and leadership).

In his attempt to unite Foucault and Marx, to write both with and against them in bringing them together, Bidet's central concept is that of metastructure. Through this concept he attempts to describe a field of possibilities and impossibilities that structures what he calls modernity, and which is irreducible to the mere relationship of exploitation characteristic of capitalism. This metastructure is a trinomial, that is, it is made up of three elements. The first is the 'discourse immediate', literally rendered herein as 'immediate discourse', which expresses a relation Bidet takes as inherent to communicational action as such (one sees the influence of John Rawls here), one between subjects who recognise each other as free and rational agents. This first element is relayed by means of two sorts of mutually presupposed 'contractual mediation' constitutive of modernity, which form the second and third elements of the metastructure. There is inter-individual contractuality, such as that operative in transactions between *market* actors; and there is central contractuality, the highest form of which is the constitution of the state *organisation* based on a social contract. The metastructure thus contains one immediate discursive relationship and two sorts of mediated, contractual relations. These latter relays are importantly connected to what he refers to as 'la coordination rationnelle-raisonable', which I've translated straightforwardly as 'rational-reasonable coordination', a phrase that expresses a distinction that he again adapts from Rawls. The 'reasonable' here pertains to someone's desiring for its own sake a social world in which people can cooperate as free and equal beings on the basis of terms accepted by all. The rational conveys a more instrumental aspect insofar as it concerns a single unified agent (or class) that bears powers of judgement and deliberation useful for achieving its own particular ends and interests. What Bidet aims to stress is that both market and organisation (inter-individual and central contractuality) belong to the dimension of the reasonable but also to the rational (hence the reason he speaks of a coordination between both terms), since they are modes of coordination which underlie an ideal of contractuality but also wherein systems of privilege can come to be established and develop mechanisms for their reproduction and extension. (For more on this I refer the reader to Alex Callinicos's account of Jacques Bidet in *The Resources of Critique,* London: Polity, 2006, pp. 35–50.)

On the issue of references, the reader is referred to the standard English editions of Marx and Foucault where possible. I have modified translations, especially of Foucault, wherever the standard English translation does not convey that aspect of the French original that Bidet aims to emphasise; I have denoted each modified translation by placing 'tm' beside the page reference. As for Bidet's own works, to which, insofar as they inform the present work, he makes frequent reference, the reader will conveniently find them all listed in the references section.

Steven Corcoran

ABBREVIATIONS

Page references in the text to the following works by Foucault use abbreviated titles as follows.

The Birth of Biopolitics	*BB*
Dits et Écrits	*DE1*, etc.
Essential Works of Foucault, 1954–1984	
Vol. 1 *Ethics: Subjectivity and Truth*	*EWF1*
Vol. 2 *Aesthetics, Method and Epistemology*	*EWF2*
Vol. 3 *Power*	*EWF3*
Foucault Live	*FL*
The History of Sexuality, Vol. 1	*HS*
Power/Knowledge	*PK*
Security, Territory and Population	*STP*
La Société punitive	*SPu*
Society Must Be Defended	*SD*

Also

The Chomsky–Foucault Debate on Human Nature, New York/London: The Free Press, 2006	*CF*

INTRODUCTION

WHY UNITE MARX AND FOUCAULT, AND HOW?

The term toward which capitalist globalisation is leading conforms to the tendency observed by Marx: a generalised commodification of goods and services, of products of knowledge, of 'labour power' itself and of all the things of nature. That this diagnostic has borne out seems to fill some of his disciples almost with pride. But the revolutions that were to come out of the very development of capitalism veered off course. And the 'new man' that entered the stage was not the much-awaited emancipated producer, but instead a subject normed and controlled on all sides, the subjugated subject of neoliberal power. In the vanguard of critique, it was Foucault who foresaw this outcome, coming thus to take over from Marx. But this he did in negative fashion, as a witness to defeat.

The future, it may be said, cannot be so precisely mapped out in advance. Indeed the attempt here proposed consists in beginning again by crossing both the Marxian and the Foucauldian heritages. For it is only in their conjunction, in their extreme tension, that they yield all their potential and discover their relative truth. This, at least, is my hypothesis.

I try to establish the conditions under which Marx and Foucault can be brought to work together in a rigorous manner, contrary to every eclectic arrangement. Naturally this cannot be managed without remainder. Foucault's work exceeds the project of Marx, and vice versa. But an essential moment of this *work in progress* falls within the framework of a sort of 'historical materialism', which each of them, in diverse ways, pertains to. I situate it chiefly in Foucault's Collège de France lectures between 1971 and 1979, which I relate back to the Marx of *Capital*.

It was during these years that two models of 'critique' and 'truth' would come head-to-head, each leading to a divergent and antagonistic political practice. This head-to-head, which Foucault's work constantly marks, and which motivates a number of his public interventions, is not confined to a situation narrowly circumscribed in space and time. It attests to a division that can be identified nearly everywhere in the world today. Let's call it, with a term taken from another era – but not without reason, as we shall see – 'contradictions among the people'. On the one hand, there are those for whom the major questions of society must be based on the processes of production and appropriation, that is, on 'exploitation', understood not simply as inequality but as a principle for capital accumulation in the hands of a minority blithe about the social and ecological content of productive labour. *For them, Marx constitutes a point of reference*. On the other, there are those for whom what is to be considered, without delay, is the constitution of the subject, the 'treatment of people by people': whether in company hierarchies, in the familial order, in relations between the sexes, between integrated majorities and those 'without part', in the administration of ethnic or sexual minorities, of the exiled and immigrants, of individuals stigmatised in terms of health or delinquency. *For them, Foucault can constitute a rallying point.* Of course, the first group claim to be just as engaged in the second register: to them nothing pertaining to what is human is foreign. The second group consider themselves the most radical critics of capitalism: of its productivist and consumerist drift. This cleavage is recurrent, however, and in my view is indicative of social criticism's emerging from structurally differentiated sites of modern society in the contemporary period. It divides and weakens the 'party' of those who call for a project of universal emancipation.

Conditions for productive collaboration have, of course, been sought from many sides. The various Marxisms, to speak only of them, have only ever lived from hybridisations linking them with associate thinkers. Throughout the generations, researchers from diverse disciplines have made such pairings – endlessly renewed – the order of the day: Marx-Weber, Marx-Keynes, Marx-Braudel, Marx-Lacan, Marx-Bourdieu, Marx-Heidegger, Marx-Rawls, Marx-Derrida … The pairing of Marx-Foucault is usually carried out today as part of a quasi-'official' programme of critical thought that refers to a triptych of 'class/race/gender'. Marx is readily mobilised for the first term, and Foucault for the other two. But by proceeding in this way, it is often difficult to go beyond the stage of an eclectic division of labour, whereby one is attributed the field, seen as easier to recognise, of exploitation, and the other is entrusted to the zones, reputedly more obscure, of domination. From this a cleavage results between these two perspectives, weakening and trivialising them both.

I will therefore attempt a high-risk undertaking, a *manœuvre de force*, in the sense that military genius gives to this expression, the aim being to comprehend both approaches together within *one and the same theoretical construction*. That is, within a 'general theory of modern society', which each approach will contribute to defining. The experiment is evidently full of pitfalls. No such account can be expected to enable us to overcome the *philosophical* dissensus between the two approaches. Concerning its *socio-theoretical* content, problems arise on both sides. The undertaking marks a rupture within the Marxist tradition. And Foucault himself would have judged it inadmissible in its very principle. For, as we know, his critique aims at a 'Hegelian' Marx, thinker of the totality and its historical unfolding to the point where social contradictions are overcome. For him, the great signifying historical ensembles, those that give their substance and their rhythm to human lives and actions, are 'apparatuses' [*dispositifs*], which are made up of heterogeneous elements, are misaligned with respect to one another, are always in movement, and are endowed with disparate speeds, intensities and orientations. They do not form a system. Heir to Nietzsche, Foucault thinks on the basis of the multitude of singular things, beings, and multiplicities that happen to come together. He conceives of order on the basis of disorder. I will take the opposite tack: I try – may you pardon my temerity – to understand disorder on the basis of order. Marxism is, as we know, haunted by such a project. It brings to light the disorder produced by capitalist order. But this does not, in my view, exhaust the field of disorder. I try to show in this regard what is missing from the tradition stemming from Marx, and why this lack leads us to turn towards Foucault. Marxism indicated the royal path, the reasonable path of struggle leading from class domination to a shared freedom-equality among all. In those 'glorious years' it would, of course, already appear that many – the mad, the ill, delinquents, deviants, foreigners and minorities of all sorts – were unable to fit into the programme. But we know what the score is in today's times of mass unemployment, disaffiliation, wandering and disintegration of community solidarities. The 'minorities' – those without part and without future or at least without horizon – have become the majority. Foucault's glory is thus not about to fade. Foucault cures us of Hegel, of that Hegel construed as being the angel of grand narrative. He will forever continue to wound us.

This contradictory relation – of affinity and repulsion between Marx and Foucault – justifies, despite the fact that more than a century separates them, the attempt to bring them together for the analysis and critique of present times, in accordance, moreover, with the respective notions they entertain of the 'critical' function of philosophy.

A fruitful encounter presupposes, in my view, the re-elaboration of each of these theoretical corpuses in the terms of 'structural' critique and 'metastructural' refoundation, that is to say that modern social 'structure' is explored on the basis of its 'metastructure'. I mean by this not its moral or political *foundation,* but instead its 'presuppositions': *the fiction that this structure presupposes and that it posits,* that is to say, that it *produces* as the *real* condition of its existence. This is the sense in which Marx undertook a critique of the 'social contract'. I have developed this project throughout several books extending over three decades and will not undertake to present it anew here.[1] It is nonetheless necessary to furnish some elementary indications.

For the interpretation of the current period, the Frankfurt school, as is well known, put forward the idea of domination through 'instrumental reason'. An echo of this can be found in Foucault, who in 1978, for example, referred in precisely this sense to 'reason as despotic light' (*DE3*/433). I put forward a consonant but, at bottom, rather different

---

[1] I take the liberty of referring to five of my earlier books: *Que faire du Capital?* (1985), *Théorie de la modernité* (1990), *Théorie générale* (1999), *Explication et reconstruction du Capital* (2004), *L'État-monde* (2011), all published by Presses Universitaires de France. [Trans. – The 1985 book has been translated into English as *Exploring Marx's Capital: philosophical, economic and political dimensions*, trans. David Fernbach, Chicago: Haymarket Books, 2009.]

The reader ought not to be surprised by the frequent references made to these works. The present work is the continuation of an ongoing account. My *metastructural theory* has the merit of existing, as one says of modest undertakings. Others apart from myself have begun to make use of it, other uses. Able to generate analytic hypotheses – in the fields of sociology, history, politics and culture – it especially welcomes criticism. Articulating 'class structure' together with 'world system', it seeks notably to clarify the development of forms of 'racial' and gender domination.

maxim:[2] 'modernity', as a historically specific social order, is to be understood in the terms of an 'instrumentalisation of reason'. Marx, it will be noted, already produced its operating schema: he both decoded the capitalist class relationship as an instrumentalisation of *commercial reason,* and defined capitalism through the exploitation of labour power transformed into a 'commodity'. In this sense, the market constitutes the metastructural presupposition that is instrumentalised in capitalist class structure. However, in my view, Marx thereby covers only half of the social field (and we will see how Foucault comes to establish himself on the other half ...). For, in reality, the 'modern class relationship' implies *two mediations: the market,* to be sure, but also, equally and correlatively, *organisation.* These are indeed, in the terms of institutionalist economy,[3] the two primary and inseparable modes of 'rational-reasonable coordination at the social level'. The instrumentalisation of reason thus consists in the fact that these two intelligent social 'mediations', market and organisation, return as 'class factors'. In other terms, in 'modern' society, the class *relationship* can be analysed as the complex combination of these two class *factors.*

---

[2] I owe a clarification of this point to Jean-Marc Durand-Gasselin, author of *L'École de Francfort,* Paris: Gallimard, 2012. As for the meaning given to 'modernity', I can only refer to the books cited above. As an initial approximation, this term refers, in keeping with the use made of it by historians, to the long period of 'modern times', and not only to the 'contemporary' period.

[3] See, for example, Oliver Williamson, *Les Institutions de l'économie,* Paris: Economica, 1994. I provide a critical analysis of this school's conceptions in my *Théorie générale,* esp. §2.2.1–2.2.2 and §7.1.1–7.1.3.

The paradox, which commentators seem never to have perceived, is that Marx is actually the one who discerned the primordial character of this duality, which, moreover, he explicitly designates as two 'mediations'.[4] He defines *the market* as an *a posteriori* equilibrium between distinct private productions, and *organisation* – the term is also his – as an *a priori* arrangement of ends and means within a production process falling under the same authority (such as the private authority of the factory, but equally the collective authority of a socialist society).[5] This duality became the pivotal point of his historico-economic theorisation. But – and this is the core criticism that I address to him – he dealt with it incorrectly precisely by transforming it into a teleological schema. He discerned in capitalist 'concentration' and 'centralisation', which are generated by competition in the *marketplace,* a correlative rise in the power of *organisation,* at the term of which there would remain – *in extremis* – only a single company per branch, or even in each nation:[6] *market* logic would thus tend to recede and ultimately yield to the logic of an order *organised* 'around concerted planning', paving the way for socialism.

---

[4] The concept of mediation (*Vermittlung*) is established in the *Grundrisse* [p. 89, of the English edition]. Marx distinguishes between two mediations, one being 'exchange value', and therefore *the market*, the other, the mode of an *organisation, 'eine Organisation…'* [p. 82 of the German edition], which ensures 'in advance' (*vorausgesetzt*) and not 'post festum' the 'social character of production'. Concerning Marx's discovery and treatment of these 'mediations', see *L'État-monde,* chapter 2.

[5] This definition is cast in *Capital,* Book 1, chapter 14, in terms of the 'division of labour in manufacturing and in society'.

[6] '[…] when the entire social capital was united in the hands of either a single capitalist or a single capitalist company', *Capital,* Vol. 1, p. 779.

In this passage to the limit, Marx in some sense places the market on the side of the past and organisation on that of the future. And this is his mistake. This is because both mediations, market and organisation, are, in modern society, structurally, which is to say, enduringly, indissociable and therefore contemporary with one another.

If both mediations can come to be instrumentalised as class factors, this is because each of them bears a potential for domination insofar as they may be subject to a socially reproducible privilege, respectively, in terms of property (on *the market*) and of 'competency' (within *the organisation*). 'Competency' here is meant not in the sense in which one *is* competent (endowed with knowledge that enables one to do …) but in the sense that one *has (received)* competency: in which one exercises *knowledge-power,* a power of leadership linked to a sanctioned knowledge. The dominant, or privileged, class thus bears two poles. The two social forces that they define – forces founded on these respective privileges, on the accumulation of social power they procure – I shall designate as that of the 'capitalists' and that of the 'competent-elites', or of 'competent agents', who are leaders through the bestowal of competence upon them. These forces both converge and are antagonistic. Now, in a one-sided way Marx defined the dominant class in *property* terms as that which possesses the means of production and exchange on the capitalist market. He missed the other pole, that of 'knowledge-power'. He had certainly foreseen the problem: after the abolition of the market, he writes in the *Critique of the Gotha Programme,* the 'enslaving subordination' of 'manual work to intellectual work' – *that is to say to knowledge-power* – will continue to persist. But he postpones the possibility of overcoming it to the distant times of the 'second phase of communism', when, duly aided by productivity, work will have ceased to be a social constraint in order to become a free activity. As we all know, this is not how things would turn out.

In reality, modern class domination is constituted in the variable relationship between *both poles* of the 'instrument-alisation of reason', hitherto designated as market and organisation. But at issue is not merely the economy. For this 'bipolarity', expressible as relations 'between-each person' [*entre-chacun*] and 'between-all' [*entre-tous*], splits in analogical fashion along its two 'faces': between what is 'rational' in the economic order (market/organisation) and what is 'reasonable' in the *juridical-political* order (inter-individual/central contractuality).[7] This entire economico-political matrix finds itself instrumentalised as part of the modern class relationship.

---

[7] It is worth noting that the expression the 'instrumentalisation of reason' becomes pertinent only once one has considered both 'faces' of what it initially designates indistinctly as 'reason': on the one hand, *economic* rationality (*Verstand,* i.e. understanding), on the other, juridico-political reasonableness (*Vernunft,* i.e. 'reason' in the strict sense). Both faces present two poles. Or again: the two poles present two faces. This is encapsulated in the various figures of the *Metastructural grid of modernity: bipolarity and bifaciality* (see *L'État-monde*, p. 55). It will be noted that the duality 'between-each-person' and 'between-all' does not equate with that of 'civil society and the state'. 'Central contractuality' does not reduce to the state: it is the presupposition of all modern 'organisation', regardless of the level in question (that of the company, for example), even the most alienating, which takes place between individuals, *presumed* free and equal.

2 FACES 2 POLES	the rational economic	the reasonable juridico-political
Between-each person	market	inter-individual contractuality
Between-all	organisation	central contractuality

It is indeed through the intersection of the perspectives defined by this 'metastructural grid' that the great programmes of the diverse 'social sciences' – economics, sociology, history, law – and equally of political philosophy were able to open up, and have continued to develop, in contradictory ways, over several centuries. On this basis we are also placed to think through an account of classes and strategies of political emancipation.[8]

Each of the terms advanced here would certainly require lengthy explanations, first and foremost that of 'organisation', which could seem incongruous in Foucauldian space, but also those of 'poles', 'faces', 'rationality', 'reasonability', 'competency', 'leaders' and so on. Marx, it will be noted, does not use the expression 'property-power', nor Foucault, at least not systematically, that of 'knowledge-power'. In my view,

---

[8] This is so, at least, with emancipation from 'structural' relations, which is to say class and state relationships. So-called 'race' relations refer us to a 'systemic' configuration, as opposed to a 'structural' one: to world-system against class-structure. In opposition to this duality, the *gender* relationship pertains to the other primary register of any social ontology. On the co-imbrication of these diverse social relations, I take the liberty of referring to chapter 5 of *L'État-monde*: 'Class, "race", sex'.

however, they are perfectly suited to expressing two concepts that play, respectively and in diverse ways, a guiding role with both these thinkers. For my part, I use them regularly in this encounter between their approaches. A theory gives the words it uses a charge that represents concepts, of which the defined content can only appear at the end of the presentation and in view of the pertinent use that can henceforth be made of them; and in so doing all it has available are words that designate things other than those the theory in question intends them to mean! I will therefore not expand upon this with further preamble.

But one can already, it seems to me, make out why we must seek to identify the relation between Marx and Foucault on the basis of this '*metastructural grid*'. In effect, it is a matter of making possible a confrontation between the 'macrological' and the 'micrological': in the first analysis, between the order of class and the order of subjects. Now, the metastructural approach – which refers to the 'class factors' presupposed in the 'class relations' – emphasises two decisive givens. On the one hand, the two 'mediations' it emphasises, market and organisation, are, as the supposed relays of an 'immediate discourse', relations *between individuals*. 'The class relationship' articulates classes via the mediation of 'class factors' that individuals articulate.

In this way, Marxian analysis, deemed 'holistic' (or 'structuralist', i.e., centred on a structured totality), finds itself able to proceed on Foucauldian 'nominalist' (individualist) terrain. On the other hand, if it is true that both class factors thus possess an analogical status, then the dominant class (which Foucault speaks about readily in reference to Marx) contains *two poles*, that of the market, governed by *proprietor-power*, and that of organisation, governed by *knowledge-power*. This being so, we will come to identify Foucault's work as one of the major wellsprings for the metastructural 'expansion' of the Marxian matrix. At another level, Bourdieu's work presents another point in case insofar as it was he who discovered 'cultural capital'. These theoreticians, among others, have developed that 'other pole', which I designate here – we revisit these terms below – as that of knowledge-power, or of 'competency', which Foucault uncovers in all institutions (hospital, prison, school, factory ...), and of which he explores certain registers, specifically those that have to do with 'bodies' and 'souls'. They illustrate the need for a broader account than that Marx bequeathed to us. Contrary to the most common practice, which consists in extending Marx's and Foucault's (or Bourdieu's) teachings to other empirical fields, the task I have set myself is to arrange them in one and the same theory, one that manifests the bipolar character of domination in the modern social order. Flowing from this, in my view, is an entire chain of consequences for the analysis and interpretation of the history of modern societies and the potentials deployed therein.

In this book, Marx and Foucault will not be treated on the same plane. I try to integrate Marx's contribution into a schema that expands his theory. With Foucault, it would make no sense to proceed in this way, since he rejected the very idea of a general theory. This will not lead me to dissolve

Foucauldian critique and analytics in Marx's conceptuality, nor Foucault's politics in Marx's. From the outset I adopt the same critical approach as regards their respective concepts. However the work required in each case is not exactly the same in scope. Foucault is a 'contemporary'. We continue to know him in the main through the (more or less) immediate reading of his works. Our knowledge of Marx proceeds from one and a half centuries of interpretations, controversies, conflicts and varied uses, both theoretical and political. In both cases, we are caught within a network of mediations, but the one connecting us to Marx is more complex and contradictory. And there is no other means of finding our way through it than to produce new readings, which do not aim finally to reach the true Marx, but to work through his concepts for an understanding of the present day.

Foucault once laid down the following challenge: 'To a Marxist who tells me that Marxism is a science, I reply: I will believe that you practise Marxism as a science the day that you will have showed me, in the name of that science, how Marx was mistaken' (*DE2*/409). I certainly refrain from trying to take up such a challenge. I do in effect seek to establish 'how Marx was mistaken' and how he might be right. But I do not do so *in the name of Marxism*, 'in the name of this [supposed] science'. I attempt a broader work of theorisation, aiming to bring Marx and Foucault together despite their antagonistic epistemologies. No post-Marxism should be sought in this, one that would finally be able to turn the page; nor should a simple neo-Marxism, some new variant of Marxism. Instead I aim at a 'meta-Marxism',[9] a *refoundation*, which involves Marxism but not merely it.

* * *

In Chapter 1, I measure the extent of the 'difference' between Foucault and Marx, the former nonetheless recognising the latter to be one of his teachers. This recognition bears on two crucial points. The first regards this mix of apparently insurmountable affinities and gaps that emerge in *Discipline and Punish* between 'disciplinary society', which is the object of his investigation, and 'class society', which he continues to presuppose in the background but never explicitly defines. The second concerns the thematic of 'governmentality', which can be contrasted to the Marxian view of the 'State', presented

---

[9] I first introduced this concept in *Théorie de la modernité* (1990). See notably the conclusion to this work, 'For a meta-Marxism', pp. 273–309. I do not today still take up all the terms I use in it. But it was the sketch of a project that has been pursued ever since. As to the term 'alter-Marxism' employed in *Altermarxisme* (PUF: Paris, 2007), a book written in collaboration with Gérard Démunil, it refers, in reference to questions raised by altermondialism, to a theorisation of the relation between class structure (until the emergence of a world class state) and world-*system*. Our respective approaches share a large affinity and many varied differences. Démunil and Lévy, who think in terms of 'mode of production', envisage a configuration with *three classes,* as in their eyes the 'cadres' form an intermediary class, increasingly so since the end of the nineteenth century. The metastructural approach, which sets itself a broader object (the 'modern form of society'), distinguishes between *two classes,* with the privileged class containing two poles, notably ever since the beginning of social modernity. I return to this in chapter 4 of *Le Néolibéralisme, Un autre grand récit*, Paris: Les Prairies Ordinaires, 2016 – 'Repériodiser les temps moderne' – in relation to the *Ancien Régime*. I base myself notably on Foucault, who attests to a broader historiography, and argue that modern organisation is not simply to be taken as a fact of capitalism. I relate it to the 'metastructural grid' of modernity.

in the lectures at the Collège de France, from 1977 to 1979. In both cases, at issue is to show how each of these partial theoretical constructions, Marx's and Foucault's, awaits the conceptual conditions of a unitary reconstruction. But also to identify what would escape from every such undertaking of unification.

In the subsequent chapters, I undertake systematically to tackle the relationship between the respective conceptualities of Marx and Foucault. I thus try to inscribe them within a broader configuration, to enable each to benefit from the effect of knowledge and critique that the other affords him. I remain as close as possible to Foucault's texts, making reference notably to the series of lectures at the Collège de France and to the philosophical insights scattered throughout *Dits et Écrits*.

Chapter 2, 'Property-power and knowledge-power', embarks on this mutual recycling of both approaches by showing the *incompleteness* of Marx's analysis, which itself does not furnish the necessary conceptual means for integrating the 'other pole' of class domination, that of 'knowledge-power'. At issue here is not to add a new wing to the Marxian edifice in order to accommodate Foucault's treasures, but instead to refound a general theory enabling us to reconstitute, on the basis of Foucauldian investigations, the 'missing links' of the theory of *Capital*.

Chapter 3, 'Marxian structuralism and Foucauldian nominalism?', investigates the meaning of this split between two philosophical choices in the terms of social science. I refer this *difference* to its expression in the dichotomy 'structure'/'*apparatuses*', which seems to govern two distinct conceptions of power, practices and social struggles. Under this broad opposition, there is a tendency to see a nominalism specific to Marx as well as a decisive contribution from Foucault to the structural analysis of modern society. At this point, however, 'weak links' appear, this time on the side of Foucault, making far more difficult the strategic elaboration of the politics from below – universalist in ambition – that each of them calls for.

Chapter 4, 'Marx's "capitalism" and Foucault's "liberalism"', examines the horizons of historical ontology to emerge from each of these theorisations. The 'productiveness' of the modern social order manifests itself very differently depending upon whether it is understood to be concerned with a mode of production or a mode of government. Both approaches, one fixed on contradictions, the other on antagonisms, nevertheless share common conceptual conditions that enable them to work together, at once against and for one another.

The final 'Elements of conclusion' seeks to answer the political question raised in this introduction. Faced with two top-down parties – one on the right, the other on the left, masked Finance versus a self-proclaimed Elite, the privileged agents of property and those of 'competence' – faced with this twin ruling oligarchy, how are we to think through this inconceivable 'third party', for which no place is anticipated on the political stage, the party of the popular multitude, which is lacking in privileges but rich in knowledge and bearing of life? 'Party' is in this case not written with a capital P, as if it were an already constituted organisation. It is meant in the sense of 'to take sides' [*prendre parti*]. For there assuredly exists a third perspective, a third principle of gathering together. *A third party.* It exists in the way that, in 1848, when no 'Communist Party' existed, a 'communist party' was given voice in a famous *Manifesto*. This is, in effect, the real issue at hand. But this party is not only one of class: it is also one of sex and of 'race'. And *it already exists*, dispersed in thousands of forms of organisations, associations, movements, initiatives, creations, indignations, revolts. It is at work in all that carries emancipation forth. Why must it continue to remain unaware of itself, prey to a frenetic and melancholic division? Will we ever really exit from that 'infantile disorder of communism'? Can the truths of Marx and those of Foucault agree with a view to forming a common strategy from below?

1

THE MARX/FOUCAULT DIFFERENCE: DISCIPLINE AND GOVERNMENTALITY

Prior to undertaking a systematic comparison, I propose to explore some analogies and discrepancies between the respective universes of Marx and Foucault, which appear through a reading of the lectures given at the Collège de France throughout the 1970s: that is, on the one hand, *Discipline and Punish,*[1] and, on the other, *Security, Territory, Population,* and *The Birth of Biopolitics.*[2] In the lectures from 1972 to 1974, on which *Discipline and Punish* draws, Foucault rather explicitly sets things in the context of a 'class' society, into which, however, he introduces a new paradigm, the 'disciplinary order'. In the lectures from 1977 to 1979, to which the latter

---

[1] *Discipline and Punish,* London: Penguin Books, 1977. The page references in the present chapter are to this edition.
[2] *Security, Territory, Population: Lectures at the Collège de France, 1977–78,* ed. Michel Senellart, trans. Graham Burchell, Houndmills, Basingstoke: Palgrave Macmillan, 2007; *The Birth of Biopolitics: Lectures at the Collège de France, 1978–79,* ed. Michel Senellart, trans. Graham Burchell, Houndmills, Basingstoke: Palgrave Macmillan, 2008.

two titles correspond, he situates himself in the field of theories and technologies of power: his approach no longer develops in terms of 'class relationships', but instead of 'relationships of government'.[3]

1.1 DISCIPLINARY SOCIETY/CLASS SOCIETY: SURVEILLANCE AND PUNISHMENT

1.1.1 Foucault's discovery of a new social order

Discipline and Punish explores the new penal and disciplinary order that appears in Europe at the end of the eighteenth century. In the case of France, the justice system of the *Ancien Régime* has been done away with, including its secret procedures and its art of extracting proofs of confession, all crowned with a spectacle of torture in which royal power is restored through terror.

The new system is grounded in public debate under the authority of a judge who is supposedly there to prevent and

---

[3] Briefly, then, I here recall Foucault's trajectory at the Collège de France over the period of interest to us and the publications connected to it. 1971–72: 'Penal Theories and Institutions', which is devoted to the worlds of *the legal system* and the *prison*; 1972–73: which continues with the same themes, under the title *On the Punitive Society*; 1973–74: *Psychiatric Power*, which deals with asylums; 1974–75: *Abnormals*, which tackles the theme of *sexuality*; 1975–76: *Society Must Be Defended*, which examines war as an analyser of the social; 1977–78: *Security, Territory and Population*; and 1978–79: *Birth of Biopolitics*. *Discipline and Punish* (1975) draws on the lectures from 1972 to 1974. *The History of Sexuality* Vol. 1 (1976) takes up themes from the lectures of 1974–75. The lectures from 1973 to 1979 were all posthumously published in French by Gallimard, and in English by Palgrave Macmillan.

correct. Execution is handed to a separate administration. Corporeal punishment is equal for all. Inflicted on a juridical subject, it consists in taking away the ultimate freedom of one's life, simply by using the horological mechanism of the guillotine. To this abstract universe of sanction corresponds a concrete individualisation of the sanctioned person. Now one no longer judges the crime but rather the criminal individual, deemed such at the outcome of a 'scientific' procedure into which the psychiatrist, as the judge of the subject's normality and of possible attenuating circumstances, would soon be introduced.

The ordeal of the prison becomes the standard form of punishment. Foucault recasts it within a broader logic, which is referred to as that of 'discipline' and is deemed to be common to barracks, factories, hospitals and schools. Military discipline, which produces a man-machine subject to a strict hierarchy, merely figures as the distillate of a phenomenon affecting all social institutions. We have here the invention of an abstract space stamped by the closure of the whole and its sub-sections, with functional quartering, the marking out of places to fix the respective terrains for each component of the group, and their comings and goings. A collective temporal rhythm is imposed on everyone, with employment and the exhaustive utilisation of time divided into standardised acts and exercises. There is a dividing up of tasks, of stages. This is not the abstraction of the *market*: it is, such is at least the argument I'm putting forward, 'another abstraction', namely *organisation*.

The 'panoptic' apparatus, utopia realised, enables the total control and monitoring of the individuals concerned. It configures the site of the normalised test, of the individual examination, medical or school, producing objective and archivable data to situate each person in his or her case or rank. It calls for an appropriate architecture, one that would come to be common to workshops, hospitals, barracks and prisons. What develops in this closed universe, away from the juridical order, is a second penal context, constituted by norms enacted from the inside, an 'infra-justice' outside of common law including corrective penalties, sanctions, punishments and rewards, distributions according to classification systems defined in accordance with the specific institution. This constitutes the instrumentalisation of the organised order by its immediate agents.

Foucault does not fail, all throughout these pages, to refer to Marx's analyses and concepts. It is clear, in his view, that such institutions are geared to the context of modern class domination – founded on economic relationships – under the aegis of the bourgeoisie. Significantly, he refers to the description of manufacturing and the factory system presented in Book 1 of *Capital*.[4] His contemporary interventions and interviews are also strewn with references to Marx. For his part, however, Foucault forged an original body of work. In this text he

---

[4] Foucault underlines this point in a talk given in Bahia in 1976. See *DE4*/186. He refers to Book 2 (and the editors repeat this erroneous formulation). In actual fact the work in question is Book 1 and its chapters on manufacture and large-scale industry.

elaborates the elements of a theorisation that has shown itself powerful enough to become the 'common sense' of contemporary critical thought. And this has occurred to such an extent that the Marxist tradition has, for some time already, been striving to appropriate him for itself. It remains to find out, however, under which conditions this 'assimilation' could be given any plausibility or coherence. Foucault, of course, presupposes a 'classist' connection between economic exploitation and political domination. But he maintains quite some distance from the properly Marxian concepts of class and state. He also marks a distinct indifference toward Marx's economic analysis and a frank hostility toward political outlooks of a Marxist type.

Marx does not have in mind the class relationship and its *reproduction,* but instead the *exercise* of 'class' (he adopts this term) power by some *individuals* over others and notably over those that institutions – private or public – have the task of controlling and setting to work. He maintains that, despite their functions of subjectivation and their repressive dimensions, the nature of these institutions is to be able to institute rational apparatuses that promote a population to higher forms of culture and power. Such is, for an essential part, the original wellspring of the social sciences. In fact in all cases, including that of prison, discipline has as its counterpart the implementation of a form of knowledge in correlation with one of power: a knowledge-power. That is, a new order of reason, which is also a new order of domination. All told, and notably as regards this ambivalence, Foucault's ambition displays something like a family resemblance to Marx's, who also sought to render capitalism its due both as force of oppression and as a factor of intellect.

1.1.2 Disciplines and class relations

My aim is to reprise these diverse points by interpreting a beautiful synoptic passage that forms the conclusion to the third part of *Discipline and Punish*. It is titled 'Discipline' (pp. 221–3) and enables us to glimpse in all its complexity the problematic relation that ties Foucault to Marx.

I begin with a line-by-line commentary on these few pages. I then compile this information into a table of observable analogies between the Foucauldian construction of 'disciplinary society' and the Marxian schema of 'capitalist society'. The hurried reader will be tempted to skip these few pages of textual analysis and go straight to the result given at §1.1.3. But it should not be forgotten that the analogies observed here do not have the value of homologies: they are only indications of problems to be identified.

Here then, in a still-disordered sequence relative to the table to be generated, the main statements from this text and my commentaries. I emphasise the most pertinent terms in Foucault's text for this analysis.

> The *panoptic modality of power* – at the elementary, technical, merely physical level at which it is situated – is not under the immediate dependence or a direct extension of the great *juridico-political structures* of a society; it is nonetheless not absolutely independent. (pp. 221–2)

The analogy is expressed in the opposition forged between a (higher) order of 'juridico-political structures' and a 'technical-physical' modality of power, which is distinguished from it. With Marx, there is a power of exploitation; with Foucault, here, a power of control.

> Historically, the process by which the *bourgeoisie* became in the course of the eighteenth century the politically dominant *class* is *masked* by the establishment of an explicit, coded and *formally egalitarian* juridical framework, made possible by the organisation of a *parliamentary,* representative regime. (p. 222)

At issue, then, is a class society in which a 'bourgeoisie' dominates politically, its power 'masked' by a 'formally egalitarian' and 'representative' juridical framework. This is a point of total proximity with Marx's perspective. It remains for us to find out, however, how the 'bourgeoisie' is distinguished from the class that Marx designates as that of 'capitalists'.

> But the development and generalisation of disciplinary mechanisms [*dispositifs*] constituted the *other, dark side* of these processes. (p. 222)

With Marx, 'the other side' of market equality, being that which makes it possible, is the mechanism of exploitation as defined in chapter 7 of *Capital*. Here we see that for Foucault it is the disciplinary apparatus that forms the other side of juridical freedom.

The general juridical form that guaranteed a system of rights that were egalitarian in principle was *subtended* by these tiny, everyday, physical mechanisms, by all those systems of micro-power that are *essentially* inegalitarian and dissymmetrical that we call the disciplines. (p. 223; tm)

In the Marxian schema, the juridical *superstructure* of egalitarian law is thus 'subtended' by a *base* of dissymmetrical material mechanisms of exploitation. From this perspective Foucault tackles an order of discipline the effect of which is 'essentially inegalitarian', just as the economic base is in Marx's work.

And although, in a *formal* way, the representative regime makes it possible, directly or indirectly, with or without relays, for *the will of all* to form the *fundamental* authority [*instance*] of sovereignty, the disciplines provide, *at the base,* a guarantee of the submission of forces and bodies. (p. 222)

The 'will of all' certainly constitutes a 'foundation' but only 'in a formal way'. This is because 'the base' is made up of disciplines that subjugate bodies. Similarly, the wage relation (the Marxian 'base') guarantees the exploitation of labour power by the capitalist who has them at his 'command' – in an order of formal liberty ensured by a parliamentary system.

The *real,* corporal disciplines constituted the foundation of the *formal,* juridical liberties. (p. 222)

The operative opposition continues to be between the 'formal' and the 'real', also referred to as the juridical and the corporal, which relates to the disciplinary 'foundation'. Foucault seems to exaggerate things as compared with Marx. Of course the reality was that neither thinker would make this play of metaphors, the disjunctions of the formal/real and superstructure/base, as their last word.

> The *contract* may have been regarded as the *ideal foundation* of law and political power; panopticism constituted the *technique,* universally spread, of *coercion.* It continued to *work* in depth on the juridical structures of society, in order to make the *effective mechanisms* of power function in opposition to the *formal* frameworks that it had acquired (*s'était donnée*). (p. 222)

Similar to Marx, the contract continues to be presupposed. This occurs within the oppositions of 'ideal foundation'/'technique' and 'freedom'/'coercion'. The contract pertains to the 'formal,' and discipline to the 'effective'. The contractual framework that class power posits ('gives itself') only exists in the conditions of 'panopticism', which 'works' it. Power's 'effectiveness' resides in this interrelation between the 'ideal' and the 'real', the nature of which remains conceptually indeterminate. It remains for us to find out if things proceed otherwise with Marx.

> The 'Enlightenment', which discovered the liberties, *also* invented the disciplines. (p. 222)

This statement confirms the preceding one: the simultaneous 'discovery' of the 'formal' and the 'real', of the 'ideal' and the 'techniques', appears not to receive a conceptual formulation in the Foucauldian framework. The *relationship* between the elements of this dualism is raised only in the vaguely additional terms of 'also', which is frequently used by this author. Nonetheless, it is this relationship that ought to concern us, as it forms the core of any future theory.

> In appearance, the disciplines constitute nothing more than an infra-law. They seem to *extend* the general forms defined by law to the infinitesimal level of singular existences; or they appear as methods of *training* that enable individuals to become integrated into these general demands. They seem to constitute the same type of law on a different scale, thereby making it meticulous and probably more lenient. (p. 222; tm)

'In appearance', says Foucault, the disciplines make one with the law, whose 'extension' they are stated to be: laws, decrees, regulations, sanctions. In Marx, things transpire in an analogical way. The contract-wage relationship appears as only one particular application of the market-contract between equals who freely exchange their products through money. In actual fact, as we see in the description of manufacturing and the factory, it determines an entire process of mechanical 'learning' that makes it possible to harness time down to its 'infinitesimal level', with far greater reach than any law is able to prescribe.

> The disciplines should be regarded as a sort of *counter-law*. They have the precise role of introducing insuperable *asymmetries* and excluding reciprocities. (p. 222)

A counter-law: they perform a reversal, a negation of legal relations. Put in Marxian terms: the wage relation performs a reversal of equality into inequality, establishing an asymmetry. The hiving off of 'surplus value' is both formally consistent with law and at the same time a reversal of law into an 'asymmetrical' disposition.

> First, because discipline creates a 'private' link between individuals, which is a relation of constraints entirely different from contractual obligation [...]. (p. 222)

Marx maintains that the wage relationship, as a class relationship, is *impersonal*. But he does not forget that it exists only by means of *inter-individual* relations established through contracts, as we are reminded in chapter 10 of *Capital*, 'The Working Day', by the 'voice of the worker' who stands up to have himself counted, saying, 'That is against our contract.' (p. 343)

> [...] the acceptance of a discipline may be underwritten by *contract*; the way in which it is imposed, the mechanisms it brings into play, the *non-reversible subordination* of one group of people by another, the 'surplus' power that is always fixed on the same side, the inequality of position

of the different 'partners' in relation to the common regulation, all these distinguish the *disciplinary link* from the *contractual link,* and make it possible to *distort* the contractual link systematically from the moment it has as its content a mechanism of discipline. (pp. 222–3)

Again, we have both registers here: discipline is at once 'accepted' and 'imposed', and thereby is the contractual link 'distorted' (we rediscover a word of Marx's: the wage contract is always 'altered').[5] The ontological status of the contract is thus to be regarded as fully pertaining to a certain social factuality: in order for it to be 'distorted' it must exist in the first place. It is not a simple appearance (printed on a form) or an illusory play of language. It arises (or is posited), however, only in a structural relation that *reproduces* inequality. Non-reversible 'subordination' is the analogue of (structurally) *reproducible* exploitation: it reproduces its conditions, it recreates a distance from itself. A 'mechanism' that reproduces itself: such is the 'structure', in which the contractual metastructure happens to be 'given'.

We know, for example, how many *real procedures undermine the legal fiction* of the work contract: workshop discipline is not the least important. (p. 223)

---

[5] *Capital,* p. 519. [Trans. – This word does not appear as such in the English edition, in which the sentence in question reads: 'Machinery also revolutionizes, and quite fundamentally, the agency through which the capital-relation is formally mediated, i.e. the contract between the worker and the capitalist.']

So again we have the opposition between the 'real' and 'fiction' – here with reference to the (Marxian) factory – fiction nonetheless being very real in its way, since it is only 'undermined'. With both Foucault and Marx, the difficulty is to produce the concept of *the relationship* between both registers of social being – reality and fiction – involved in the 'apparatus'. What, then, is the reality of this fiction? Such is the difficulty we have to tackle.

> Moreover, whereas the juridical systems define *juridical subjects* according to universal norms, the disciplines characterise, classify, specialise; they distribute along a scale, around a *norm, hierarchise* individuals in relation to one another, and, if necessary, *disqualify* and invalidate. (p. 223)

In the analysis of Marx, who relies on the 'critical economists' that preceded him and on work inspectors, hierarchy within the enterprise is strongly stressed.[6] Yet it remains secondary as regards the *essential*: the division of *wage earners/capitalists*, that is, the *class relationship* that defines his theory of exploitation and accumulation. Hierarchy appears as a *corollary* to the capitalist system. Foucault turns it into a theoretical object that is to be considered for itself. In it, he discerns a new order of power, one of 'knowledge-power', as distinct from proprietor-power. He thus opens up a new conceptual register, as averred

---

[6] Ibid., pp. 449–50.

by the fact that his account applies to all social institutions. The capitalist enterprise, in which managers cease to be the mere *representatives* of the power of the proprietor and exercise a specific power, is only a particular case. What, on the other hand, brings both accounts closer is the discovery of a mechanism of invalidation and exclusion of a structural nature. The mechanism of the capitalist *market,* analysed by Marx, excludes its 'reserve army'; it 'invalidates' labour power not suited to making profit. Similarly, according to Foucault, the hierarchical apparatus of *organisation*, regardless of the institution considered, 'disqualifies', 'invalidates'; it produces those it *excludes.*

> In any case, in the space and during the time in which they exercise their control and bring into play the asymmetries of their power, they effect a *suspension* of the law that is never total, but is *never annulled* either. (p. 223)

The order of law remains firmly in place. But it is placed in parentheses: there are places of right and places of non-right. This distinction between places and times is essential. Just as is the fact that labour power is only sold 'for a determinate time', but also in a specific place, that of production, in which extra-juridical relations of force intervene, but which does not encompass the entirety of existence. So, conceiving of two space-times in terms of exteriority, one ruled by law and the other saturated with non-right, is obviously not enough. Both Foucault and Marx work to construct the concept of the relation between both these registers.

> Regular and institutional as it may be, the discipline, in its mechanism, is a *'counter-law'*. And, although the universal juridicism of modern society seems to fix limits on the exercise of power, its universally widespread panopticism enables it to operate, on the underside of the law, a machinery that is both immense and minute, which supports, reinforces, multiplies the asymmetry of power and undermines the limits that are traced around the law. (p. 223)

Foucault's central theme is again reiterated here: disciplinary regulation is not the pursuit of an order of law by other means. Marx also showed that the wage relation is not analysable in the simple terms of a continuation of market law, of a generalised state of right, but that it establishes mechanisms which are by no means juridical, such as, for instance, those designed to intensify work. But Foucault's field of analysis overruns Marx's and extends to the entirety of social life.

> The *minute* disciplines, the panopticisms of every day may well be *below* the level of emergence of the *great apparatuses* and the *great political struggles*. But, in the genealogy of modern society, they have been, with the *class domination* that traverses it, the political counterpart of the juridical norms according to which power was redistributed. (p. 223).

For Foucault, in contrast with Marx, 'class domination' (the class structure) does not *define* 'modern society'. It nevertheless 'traverses' it from end to end. We must learn how to discern these minute and everyday facts, situated *'below'* (at the base of) great politics, where the 'great struggles' (*class struggles*: such is how Foucault intends it here) revolve around 'great apparatuses', which seize hold of the great juridical principles by which power 'is distributed'. The singular occurs in correlation with the global.

> Hence, no doubt, the importance that has been given for so long to the small techniques of discipline, to those apparently insignificant *tricks* that it has invented, and even to those *'sciences'* that give it a *respectable* face; hence the *fear* of abandoning them if one cannot find any substitute; hence the *affirmation* that they are at the very *foundation* of society, and an element in its equilibrium, whereas they are a series of mechanisms for *unbalancing* power relations definitively and everywhere; hence the persistence [*one's* persistence] in regarding them as the humble, but concrete form of every *morality*, whereas they are a set of physico-political techniques. (p. 223)

This provides a subtle distribution of concepts, set in their respective places and topological relations. Disciplinary mechanisms pertain to a practice (of class, in a sense to be defined), which is 'cunning' and has a strategic aim: they are mechanisms *'for'* unbalancing. 'One' nevertheless has every reason to fear that they will be ineffective if *one* fails to mobilise the 'knowledge' making it possible to convey them as being 'at the foundation' of a rational balance, as administrating an 'immanent' morality. Such an (interpellative) claim should be considered in its illocutionary triplicity, as defined by Habermas: it claims to be simultaneously (1) *true* and (2) *just*. As to the third term of the illocution, which concerns (3) the authentic *identity* of the speaker, it is expressed here in terms of 'one'. It is this discursivity immanent to the class relationship that remains to be explored in both Marx and Foucault.

> To return to the problem of legal punishments, the prison with all the *corrective* technology at its disposal is to be *resituated* at the point where the codified power to *punish* turns into a disciplinary power to *monitor*; at the point where the *universal* punishments of the law are applied *selectively* to certain individuals and always the same ones; at the point where the redefinition of the *juridical subject* by the penalty becomes a *useful training* of the criminal; at the point where the law is *inverted* and passes *outside* itself, and where the counter-law becomes the *effective* and institutionalised content of the juridical *forms*. What generalises the power to punish, then, is not the universal consciousness of the law in each juridical subject; it is the regular extension, the infinitely minute web of panoptic techniques. (p. 224)

Here we arrive at a sort of recapitulative conclusion, which is dialectical in consonance. The formal juridical order, in which the 'universal consciousness of law' is posited, 'is inverted':

counter-law becomes its 'effective', *wirklich,* content. Or – another metaphor – it exits itself, just like a Hegelian inside can *be* only through its 'outside'. This marks the passage from the 'universal' to the particular: from a 'juridical subject' identical to all others to the (bad) subject to be forced within the norm. And at issue is a class dialectic that strikes 'always the same people' with the aim of producing a 'useful' subject (a utility still to be defined). The panopticon, which sums up the whole, metonymically figures the *knowledge-power* at work here. For this *general* concept of *knowledge-power* is precisely the one by which the Foucauldian analysis manages to unify the field it discovers. It is this concept that will bear articulating together with that other power, not that of competence but of property, which the Marxian account identifies.

1.1.3 Analogical table Foucault/Marx

In the table, I very provisionally summarise the set of analogies as well as the resemblances and differences evident in our respective constructions of Marx and Foucault. The table must naturally be taken with the utmost caution. For what remains to be specified is that content of each of the terms arranged in this space, as well as to explore their possible interrelations both in each author's work and from one problematic to another. This topological exercise merely aims at drawing out a set of questions to be addressed. The ultimate stake here is not to know what sort of *comparison* is possible between Marx and Foucault, but instead what sort of re-elaboration is required to determine the conditions under which their concepts could harmonise in a single theory: an overall theory of the modern

Foucault			Marx
Contractual fiction	– 'imagined contract' – 'fiction', 'appearance' – 'formal framework' – 'ideal foundation' – 'confessable'	Super-structure	Contractual fiction – state (social contract) – market (wage exchange)
'juridico-political structures'	– 'subject of right' – 'will of all' – 'parliamentary regime'		Juridical institutions Political institutions
'inversion' *The disciplines*:	– 'distort' – 'work' – 'disequilibrate' – 'invert' – 'twist' – 'subtend'		The wage apparatus overturns the market contract into capitalist exploitation. It puts labour power at the disposal of the capitalist, whereby the contract is 'distorted'.
DISCIPLINES **Control** – space – time – the tasks **Means** – surveillance – normalisation – sanctions – examinations **Panopticon**	**What the disciplines achieve** – 'classified subjects' – 'hierarchised subjects' – 'irreversible subordination' – 'essentially inegalitarian' – 'insurmountable dissymmetries' **What the disciplines are** – the 'base', the 'foundation' – 'technical processes' – 'effective mechanisms'	Infra-structure	**CLASS RELATIONS** **Relations of production** reproduce class relations: exploitation, inequality and dependence **The productive forces** Productive techniques that also transform the worker

form of society. Foucault strongly rejects any such prospect. The thesis that I put forward is that he nonetheless provides powerful aids toward elaborating such a theory, especially insofar as he enables a more precise definition of the limits of this sort of project.

Not all of these terms are to be placed on the same plane, as they do not present the same level of conceptualisation. Foucault is a master of chiaroscuro: the vague background of law is given only to offset that which concerns him most, namely the disciplines. Despite the semantic uncertainty remaining in this first approach, we begin to see in outline the conditions of an encounter between these two sets of problematics. Even so, it seems that the Marxian and Foucauldian concepts are actually so heterogeneous in nature as to be unable to be connected without an overarching theoretical refoundation.

1.2 CIVIL SOCIETY AGAINST CLASS STATE: THE COLLÈGE DE FRANCE LECTURES OF 1977–79

In 1977, a time, in France and in Europe more broadly, when the Eurocommunist wave springing from 1968 was beginning to peter out, a time when – in the wake of a 'new economy' – the noisy cohort of 'new philosophers' was starting to assert itself, Foucault set out to address in his lectures at the Collège de France what was being heralded as the 'new politics'.[7]

---

[7] On the content of these lectures see *Security, Territory, Population* and *The Birth of Biopolitics,* referenced above in note 2 of this chapter. For an elaboration of the 'course context', of its political and theoretical backdrop, the reader may refer to Michel Senellart's precious account (*STP*/369–91).

Foucault had hitherto limited himself to studying particular institutions: prisons, hospitals, asylums, schools, barracks. He now moved, as he put it, from these 'sectorial techniques' on to 'great politics', on to the 'technology of state power', and even proffered a live commentary on the proposals made by the then leaders, Raymond Barre and Valéry Giscard d'Estaing [prime minister and president, respectively], drawing on precedents from the eighteenth to the twentieth centuries. He thus presented neoliberalism as the present stage of liberalism. Fewer than ten years after '68, at the end of a decade of social struggles and wars of liberation that could have seemed, throughout the world, to herald the twilight of capitalism, Foucault announces its rebirth.

How does he position himself in relation to 'liberalism'? Ought we to hear his discourse as a *praise* of liberalism and as offsetting the Marxian critique of political economy? (§1.2.1). To the controversial question of knowing what political position Foucault is taking in these lectures, I prefer that of knowing which literary genre, which scientific genre, he is practising in them.[8] Not insignificantly, we might note that Foucault proceeds, as Marx also does, in the form of a *grand narrative* (§1.2.2). The difference between these narratives consists not only in the difference of their respective subjects, but also in the

---

[8] These lectures (similar to Marx's unpublished writings) place us before a process of research, a hazardous process, the doubts and uncertainties of which we must weigh up, and which are sometimes given trenchant and polemical formulations. The summary that Foucault draws up of his lectures of 1979 (*DE3*/819–25), which is done after the fact and contains some revisions, stakes out a greater distance to liberalism.

fact that the Foucauldian narrative, in contrast with the Marxian one, ultimately presents us with a grand *tableau* (§1.2.3).

1.2.1 *Praise* versus *critique* of the political economy?

Bearing in mind that Marx essentially strove to provide a '*critique* of the political economy' (as the subtitle of *Capital* indicates), it is striking to note that Foucault, who is in part interested in the same authors – namely the English physiocrats and liberals – seems, conversely, to engage in some sort of *praise*. Marx examines the *economic theories* of the above-mentioned authors, Foucault the *policies* they inspire. Yet the material that Marx and Foucault work through is the same, namely economico-political discourses. Their approaches, however, are at loggerheads. Marx seeks to show that the object of capitalist production is not, in the terms of Adam Smith, the 'wealth of nations', concrete wealth, or use-value, but instead abstract wealth, or surplus-value. Foucault, by contrast, aims to show how the liberal political economy takes aim at life, the population, concrete wealth and the power of society. Marx, in the first section of Book 1, presents the market model, defined as a rational logic of production of social wealth. The 'law of value' – according to which commodities are exchanged as a function of the labour time socially required for their production – tends to be imposed in a situation of competition, ensuring the optimal allocation of resources and the maximisation of productivity.[9]

---

9 On this interpretation of the 'law of value' – and its justification – I take the liberty of referring to my *Explication et reconstruction du Capital*, pp. 51–6.

But in Section 3 he goes on to say that we cannot stop at this abstract level of analysis, since, in the *capitalist* market, labour power itself functions as a productive commodity: it produces surplus value. Henceforth competition does not revolve around the production of commodities as use-values, but instead around profit maximisation. The aim of capitalist production, of the capitalist entrepreneur, via the production of commodities, is therefore not 'wealth', but profit, or abstract wealth. Marx does not deny that the 'capitalist mode of production' produces infinitely more wealth than those that preceded it. Instead, he maintains that the dynamic of capitalist accumulation, grounded in exploitation, is unable to be adequately accounted for in these terms, because its logic is that of surplus value. He elaborates, contrary to the liberals, the concepts of difference and of contradiction between wealth and profit. And from there he goes on to interpret the historical development of capitalism.

It is naturally possible to try to articulate both these discourses. Marx does not forget that, if the logic of capitalists is profit, abstract wealth, profits will only be made on condition that they sell their commodities, and thus that the latter are endowed with a pertinent use-value, concrete wealth (which I analyse below in §4.1.2 as the 'productive contradiction of capital'). He makes this question the central focus of his study on reproduction, crisis and accumulation, and studies the contradictions of the systems only on the basis of their relative rationality. Yet he did not ever provide a conceptual elaboration of the demand that flows from it, namely 'governmental' constraint, that is to say *hegemonic* constraint in the Gramscian sense, which incites the dominant class to respond – to a degree not yet specified – to the demands of the society. Nor did he consider the multiform network of social knowledges and sectorial practices through which such a power is exercised ... Perhaps it is enough to add, then, that Foucault clearly grants Marx the fact that behind liberal discourse there is also exploitation, replete with its coercive apparatuses. And also that he provides what is still missing in order to account for the eminently historical productivity of capitalism: the analysis of the knowledge-powers that impel it. With little effort, we could thus have 'Foucault with Marx'.

Combining both approaches in this way nonetheless runs the risk of occulting what it is that separates them, namely what is evident in the gaps between each of their 'grand narratives'.

1.2.2 The Foucauldian grand narrative and the neoliberal question

Foucault sets out a 'genealogy of the modern state and of its apparatuses on the basis of a history of governmental reason' (*STP*/354). This *genealogy* is developed across a series of three successive historical 'moments', which structure the account.

The entry into political modernity proceeds with the triumph, in Renaissance times, of the figure of *Sovereignty*, which is exercised through law over subjects: this is 'the state of justice', ruled by 'the system of the legal code with a binary division between the permitted and the prohibited (*STP*/5).

The Peace of Westphalia (1648) signals the entry into the classical age, featuring the rapid expansion of the *administrative state* and the development of disciplinary institutions. This is the time of the mercantilists, who endorse a volontarist export industry, which guarantees the state the financial windfalls required to establish its power. The 'balance between states' (*STP*/298–9) constrains each of them to conform to this exigency. In the purview of its own power, the 'police state', in the sense that the term *Polizei* acquires in the eighteenth century, seeks to promote the population's 'life' and 'happiness' (*EWF1*/71). The 'reason of state' grounds resources and populations in 'statistics' (*STP*/274). Beyond legal and judicial paths, one thus seeks to prevent and correct through the use of the appropriate 'detective, medical and psychological' techniques (*STP*/5). The modern state thus becomes a great machinery that functions as a 'permanent *coup d'État*' (*STP*/340): ordinances, interdictions, instructions, regulations, the local discipline of the workshop, the school and the army. The demand for a limitation of state power comes to be heard, from the inside, as a demand expressed by jurists in terms of natural law and the social contract.

From 1750 on, the figure of *Government* emerges together with the physiocrats. The political economy is its main technology of power. Henceforth its foremost target is not international trade but national production. The market, as a logic of production, is its 'site of veridiction'. In contrast with the state of sovereignty, which operates through law, through right, through 'jurisdiction', liberal governmentality in effect functions through 'veridiction': through the *truth* of supposed 'natural' mechanisms (*BB*/31–2). It entails specific juridical presuppositions of freedom, not those of freedom in general, but rather 'freedom of the market, freedom to buy and sell, the free exercise of property rights, freedom of discussion, possible freedom of expression and so on' (*BB*/63). And it is through both these means, the economic and the juridical, that the self-limitation of governmental reason is accomplished, against the limitlessness of the police state. *On the other side,* the multiple domain of governmental intervention develops, but in a more flexible form than in the previous era: it proceeds with a search for 'security' based on the acceptable, the probable, the average and implies procedures of 'normation' (*STP*/57–9). As in the example of smallpox inoculation, a preventative technical procedure designed to induce and control, it operates in the domain of the probable and the generalisable. In this way the concepts of 'case', 'risk', 'crisis', etc., emerge. More than ever before, all this takes the 'population' as its context, where by population is meant a set of living beings that, Foucault says, Marx only succeeded in 'circumventing' via that of 'class' (*STP*/77).

This 'history of political reason' does not stop there, however. On 24 January 1979, Foucault, passing over Keynesianism, which he refers to as a 'crisis of liberalism' (*BB*/69), sets down to study a new option that then emerges with a din: *neoliberalism.* Foucault understands the latter as a response to this 'crisis'. He explains that Hayek and others explore this 'new apparatus of governmentality' from the 1930s on.[10] However, it is the

---

[10] A presentation of the history of neoliberal ideas that is inspired by Foucault can be found in Pierre Dardot and Christian Laval, *The New Way of the World: On Neoliberal Society,* London: Verso, 2014 [2009].

situation that arises in Germany, year zero, that provides the ground for experimentation. The total decomposition of the previous economic order effects a *tabula rasa*, leading to a different formulation of the problem: the market is approached not as a *fact of nature*, but as an *objective* to be realised and universalised. The market is a 'project of society': society is to become a market. The state, ceasing to pursue concrete ends, to work through measures and correctives, is thus to limit itself to fixing the rules of the game, allowing economic actors to play it out amongst themselves. In France, Giscard D'Estaing was first to take up this doctrine in opposition to the previous compromises of Keynesianism. Once every idea of a plan, of substantial intervention in the economy, has been ruled out, a 'state of right' comes to be established that is exclusively regulated according to 'formal principles' (*BB*/171) required by the market. We thus are obliged to talk here of an 'economico-juridical order', in which the 'juridical informs the economic' (*BB*/163; tm). The reverse is also applicable, since at issue are 'the necessary rules of right in a society regulated on the basis of and in terms of the competitive market economy' (*BB*/160). The idea is thus dismissed that employment could be an objective or equality a socially pertinent category: the 'social question' comes to be regulated, outside of law and in the margins of the economy, as a *moral* question, a question of the morally acceptable level of poverty. American neoliberalism takes a step further still with its 'theory of human capital' (*BB*/219–29), wherein work is taken as a capital, one that the worker is supposed to consider from the viewpoint of 'the optimal allocation of rare resources to alternative ends'.[11] This brilliant 'epistemological transformation' (*BB*/222) would, we know, come to take over the entire social field, from the conjugal to the penal. In little time, it would become the guiding principle of a globalised economy. It should be recognised that, on the side of the critical tradition, Foucault is one of the first to take the measure of this event.

Foucault does not fail to mark a distance towards 'modes of action that are at least as compromising for freedom' as those 'that *one* wants to avoid', whether it be 'communism, socialism, national-socialism, or fascism' (*BB*/69). (I emphasise again this 'one', which connotes a recurrent uncertainty as to the subject of the enunciation.) Of this 'state-phobia' (*BB*/76), he mentions the dangers (example of genetics, *BB*/228), as well as the evidently unfortunate 'immediate political connotations' (*BB*/230). But, he adds, 'this lateral political product' does not permit us to remain at the level of simple 'denunciation'. This would be 'mistaken and dangerous' as regards the many phenomena that these analyses have shed light on. Foucault here mentions issues as diverse as the educational investments of parents, the tendency of the rate of profit to fall, Japanese growth and growth in general and the possible burgeoning of the Third World. This is the direction, he observes, in which 'economic', 'social', 'educational' and 'cultural policies' are

---

11 Foucault specifies that this runs counter to Marx, who he alleged was all about 'abstract work' (*BB*/221). In saying this, Foucault takes his liberties. His aim is to reveal the capacity of work to produce useful things (what *Capital* defines precisely as 'concrete work') to be a form of capital. As is well known, this is the idea that Marx's 'critique' seeks to undermine.

being oriented … He underlines 'the effectiveness of neoliberal analysis and programming' (*BB*/233), which are also, he points out, to be taken together with 'their coefficient of threat'. He sees in neoliberalism the 'theme-programme of a society in which there is an optimisation of systems of difference, in which a field is left open to oscillatory processes and in which minority individuals and practices are tolerated […]'. (*BB*/259–60)

This grand narrative aims to define, or so it seems, the ultimate political stake as being about the 'survival of capitalism', about the possible invention of a 'new capitalism'. Delivered with extraordinary pathos, Foucault's sharp address to his audience, a large number of whom were doubtless ill-converted from the Marxism of the '68 years, exclaims: if there is only a single 'logic of capital', that of profit, its end inscribed in advance in 'definitive impasses', then before long 'capitalism will no longer be' (it being implied: as you had believed!). However, if instead (it being implied: as I will show you!) capitalism is deployed according to a diversity of spirits and rationalities, then what is opened to it is a whole 'field of possibilities' (*BB*/165–6). His discourse, as we see, is entirely directed toward a *future* of capitalism. At issue, therefore, is not merely 'liberalism' as an art of governing based on the capitalist economy, but instead the history and the future of capitalism itself.

If Foucault is philosophically sceptical, as Paul Veyne insists he is,[12] he is nonetheless not prevented from having

---

[12] Paul Veyne, 'Un Archéologue sceptique', in Didier Éribon (ed.) *L'Infréquentable Michel Foucault,* Paris: EPEL, 2001, pp. 19–59.

political opinions, the examination of which presents a theoretical interest for whoever aims to understand his work. One cannot be merely content to say that he examines neoliberalism as a 'utopia' worthy of being studied.[13] Indeed his study programme actually takes as its focus the 'real neoliberalism' then emerging. And, as we see, he makes political judgements concerning it. But the question of his personal stance is not the one we will dwell on. Instead, to adopt Weber's terms, we will investigate what relates to the responsibility of the 'scholar' and not to the 'politician'; that is, both to his work as a historian – the way in which he understands the historical process – and to his critical elaboration as regards our historical actuality.

Two types of question arise about this form of narrative.

On the plane of history, Foucault underlines that the novelties introduced by liberalism do not usher out the former techniques of government. The facts of the 'police' that he describes in his 1978 lectures and the facts of 'discipline' analysed in the 1972 lectures are both part of the liberal context. These technologies, in concert with those of 'government by political economy', are constitutive of the era of liberalism;[14]

---

13 This is the interpretation provided by Geoffroy de Lagasnerie in *La Dernière Leçon de Foucault,* Paris: Fayard, 2012. See notably, p. 41ff. In so doing the author connects Foucault to Hayek. He salutes the 'neoliberal deconstruction of "monist" conceptions', p. 107. How does he not see, however, that neoliberalism, which conceives of things in the terms of the market, represents in its way the very summit of monism?

14 Moreover, it will be noted that in the domain of the 'police' his investigation is the most innovative and valuable to date. Pierre Lascoumes convincingly develops the following hypothesis: 'Michel Foucault's main contribution to political science resides in the shift that he effectuated

they pertain – at least according to an expression that had been familiar to him for a long time – to the same 'class power'. But how does all this operate together? A decisive problem might indeed stem from the division of this governmental technology in the 'liberal era' into these two poles, one of which operates on the *market,* which it guides in following it, the other taking charge of the population by means of *organisation.*[15] According to which *structural* constraint does this hold together socially? That is to say, according to which *class relationships?* It is not clear, as we shall see, that the Foucauldian problematic allows us to get the measure of this bipolarity, which he nonetheless contributes powerfully to bringing to light.

On the plane of social critique, it may be somewhat surprising not to see him engage more prominently in a substantive evaluation of these claims to govern rationally. What occurs, notably in neoliberalism, in the *life* of populations? And what are we to make of the relation between law and the economy? Neoliberalism is tackled as a technology that intends both to *unite right and the economy* and to *separate the economy from the social.* This amounts to generating a *law separated from the social, which is also to say from the political.*

---

from the theorisation of the state to a comprehension of it from the angle of its practices, that is to say, its governmentality defined as a specific mode of exercise of power.' See his 'La Gouvernementalité: de la critique de l'État aux technologies du pouvoir', in *Foucault, usages et actualités (Le Portique,* Nos. 13–14), 2004, p. 169. He emphasises Foucault's reference to cameral science, 'the crucible of contemporary public policies', p. 174.
[15] In accordance with the cleavage sketched in the Introduction and which is examined in Chapter 2.

How can Foucault, so engaged in political critique, leave all this in suspense? His claim to 'perspectivism' seems to lead him to take the successive perspectives of those he speaks about, in keeping with the successive ages of political reason. But how can we think through these diverse perspectives together?

1.2.3 Foucault's grand tableau:
civil society and the arts of governing

Foucault does not fail, however, to underline that these three figures of governmental reason – sovereignty, state, government – which emerge more or less successively, do not exclude each other but are made up of one another, add on to one another, and have to be treated as a 'triangle' (*STP*/107), that is to say, as forming together a complex figure of modern political rationality. From then on, the problem will be, it seems to me, to know to what extent and how Foucault manages to think through their contemporaneity, that is to say their structural unity.

In actual fact his investigation is not organised around this 'triangular' form. It concentrates progressively on the claims of liberalism to unite law and economy. On 28 March 1979, leaving neoliberalism to one side, he returns to studying classical liberalism and to the programme he mentioned at the start of the lecture course: to think together the twin questions of political right and of economic utility. He underlines immediately that in 'liberalism' – to which he then gives an extremely broad meaning – there are two paths for thinking through this unity: 'the revolutionary approach', which sets out from human rights, and 'the radical utilitarian approach', which is oriented toward the independence of the governed (*BB*/41). But it is far and away the latter – the one that has 'held out', where the other has 'receded' (*BB*/43) – that will inspire him in the remaining lectures.

The aim, he says, is no longer to have to 'divide the art of governing into two branches, the art of governing economically and the art of governing juridically'. Now, this was precisely the problem raised by the young Marx, for whom, as we know, the aim was to overcome the split between the 'bourgeois' and the 'citizen', that is to say, between *market* economics and the *juridico-political* order. This project would stay with him always, as we see at the start of *Capital* in Section 1, which is devoted to the logic of market production, in which the account articulates categories that are at once economic and political, providing a rigorous formulation of the 'economico-political' that Foucault ascribes to the liberals.

The 'critique' to which he then submits it in Section 3, which is devoted to capital (his 'critique of the political economy'), shows the mechanism by which this 'separation between the bourgeois and the citizen is performed' and why it is never total (and why the 'voice' of the waged and Chartist citizen – given expression in chapter 10 – who fights for entirely different 'legislation' cannot be stifled). In presenting the liberal ambition to overcome the split between *homo oeconomicus* and *homo juridicus,* Foucault declares his interest in an analogical project. But he takes the problem from the other side. Each thinker gives responses that may elicit reservations. Marx wants to abolish the economic order of the *market,* which the liberals see as the measure of the juridical order. And he imagines that *organisation* (organised on the basis of concerted planning among all) announces the primacy of political democracy. Foucault has us understand that the 'split' has already been effectively overcome, not beyond capitalism, but under the aegis of liberalism, insofar as it sets itself 'a new field of reference': 'civil society' (*BB*/295).

Marx, for whom the modern economy is not the market but the *capitalist* market, confronts the 'bad infinite' of capital, its limitless tendency toward abstract wealth. By contrast, Foucault, in liberal mode, has his sights permanently set on the limitless tendency of the state to veer towards the most concrete forms of power. By conforming itself to the spontaneity of a supposedly natural economic game, the specificity of which is to be open and non-totalisable, government is 'self-limiting' – a key word. In this way, it respects the 'rules of right' by respecting the 'specificity of the economy' (*BB*/296). This illustrates for us the concept of 'civil society'.

Concerning this concept, Foucault, basing himself on Ferguson, actually supplies two more or less tangled approaches: one, I would say, in terms of *Gemeinschaft*, community, and the other in terms of *Gesellschaft*, society – two figures of which the supposed fusion seems to furnish the key to the problem. Civil society is to be understood as the form of concrete life of a *historical* community, which both is a *spontaneous* symbiosis of disinterested interest and is traversed by the interested relations of the economy. It is thus made up of relations that are 'neither purely economic nor purely political' (*BB*/308) and that are part of a relation of 'subordination' (*BB*/309), that is, a relation between governors and the governed. The problem to be resolved is about how to 'govern according to the rules of right' in a 'space of sovereignty' [...] inhabited by economic subjects' (*BB*/294–6). Well, civil society, when precisely understood as a specifically modern concept of *society*, provides us with a solution insofar as it 'indexes' 'right to the market economy': it is 'the juridical economy of a governmentality indexed to the economic economy' (*BB*/296; tm). 'Indexation' refers to the economic (i.e. market) relation that *indicates* what a juridical relation is properly speaking, namely an order of right. The market becomes *the index* of right.

But Foucault, one will not fail to note, had already characterised liberalism in almost the same terms just some weeks prior.[16] It is accordingly appropriate to ask what it is that distinguishes neoliberalism from liberalism *tout court*. What allows this problematic vagueness is that the concept of civil society, once expressed in the terms of the market economy, paradoxically ignores the other dimension of class power – that of organisation – which is equally accomplished as an economy: at issue here is not only 'discipline' in the restricted sense of *Discipline and Punish*, but also the 'police' that mobilises it in the service of a 'reason of state' and that is concretised in the management of the 'life' of the population through hospitals, schools and state bodies of prediction and

---

[16] See the reference given above (*BB*/160–2).

control. These 'apparatuses' do not (at least not entirely) stem from a market economy; they nonetheless constitute an 'economy', in the proper sense of being founded upon labour that produces services and other use-values. Now, by invoking 'civil society', Foucault remains wedded to the liberal conceptual framework, since he surreptitiously reduces the economy to the market, the nature of which, accompanied by corrective 'interventions', remains mysterious insofar as he examines neither its social determinants nor its conditions of justification. He seems to take on board the fiction according to which right and economy translate into one another, from the moment that obeying right is tantamount to adhering to the economy, and vice versa ... with the codicil according to which the (market) economy, because it is a fact of nature (liberal version) or a demand of reason (neoliberal version), is precisely what supplies us, in the first instance at least, with an index of right.

Now, this is precisely the theoretical landscape that Marx develops in Section 1, Book 1, of *Capital*, which is nothing other than an account of a pure 'civil society' according to the juridico-economic features of a 'market economy'.[17] In Section 3, he then elaborates a 'critique' of the idea that modern society is thus built upon *a juridical order of exchanges*, showing it to be a 'fiction', a *presupposition*, of the capitalist market order.

---

[17] In metastructural terms, as defined in the Introduction (note 7), this is a social order understood according to its two 'faces', economic and *politico-juridical,* but conceived in terms of a *pure* market, that is to say, devoid of its other pole, namely *organisation.*

It is a very *real* fiction, nonetheless, one endowed with effects (what is more, contradictory ones). But does Foucault credit liberalism with more than this? It might be suspected that he does when he shows how the liberal claim to conform to a natural order is swept aside by the neoliberal claim that it has to do with a fiction, since in actual fact some such rational order has yet to be constructed. One senses that an important part of the confrontation between Marxism and liberalism will bear on the relation between reality and fiction.

As we see, it appears rather difficult to find in the concept of 'civil society', defined by market relations, a global solution to the problems of political power that Foucault is trying to tackle. Moreover, at the end of his last lecture he himself puts forward, in a sort of final reversal and as the ultimate lesson to be taken from the talks, a general tableau in which the three elements of the 'triangle' – sovereignty, state, government – are presented as the interplay of *three arts of governing*. As he puts it, 'You see that in the modern world, in the world we have known since the nineteenth century, a series of governmental rationalities overlap, lean on each other, challenge each other and struggle with each other: an art of government according to truth, an art of government according to rationality of the sovereign state, an art of government according to the rationality of economic agents' (*BB*/313). Only at this point does it beome clear that his approach exceeds the framework of 'classical liberalism', since 'nationalist politics' and 'state politics' – and even 'something like Marxism' he says, 'pegged [...] to the rationality of history progressively manifesting itself as truth' – all fall within the same 'political debate' (ibid.). 'Our rationality' is broadened, by this ecumenical peroration, into diverse rationalities.

It nonetheless remains that Foucault gives to what he designates most specifically as 'liberalism' a privileged position. Were there any doubt about this, the reader should refer to the twice-repeated expression on the last page of the lecture series, according to which liberalism, in aligning itself with the rationality of 'economic subjects', and of subjects 'as subjects of interest' (interest in the broadest meaning on the term, it is true), founded an 'art of government on the rational behaviour of those who are governed', an 'art of government on the rationality of the governed themselves' (*BB*/312). The encounter between Foucauldianism and Marxism thus announces itself as a severe test.

But, despite everything, the interest of the Foucauldian grand narrative is that it reduces to a grand tableau in which these diverse social logics cohabit and clash – in contrast with that of Marx, for whom the ultimate lesson (despite the taboos that weigh on the exegesis) is truly that the hour will come when concerted planning among all will come to replace the capitalist market order, and this will occur through the abolition of private property and the market, which are its ultimate conditions. It is perhaps equally difficult to determine if Marx would have, had the situation presented itself, pushed to this extremism as it is to know the degree to which Foucault recognised himself in the liberalism of which he spoke. But, if the schema of liberal governmentality is related to that of administrative governmentality, to which *it is added*, if the tableau of civil society is related to that of the disciplines, we can understand how the Foucauldian composite landscape furnishes the elements necessary to the defining of this resilient bipolarity, that of a modernity that pertains both to the market and to organisation.

In this first chapter, we have taken only the first steps. As regards Marx, I have yet to engage in any critique. Instead I have strived to show his potential affinities with the concerns Foucault adopts. As regards Foucault, I have primarily sought to signal the uncertainties of a discourse that has neither the same ambition, nor the same systematic demands, as it stands opposed to every idea of 'system', but also to highlight an analytical and conceptual renovation with the ability, it seems to me, to trigger a crisis in, or reset in motion, the heritage of Marx. This is the stake of the following chapters.

2

PROPERTY-POWER AND KNOWLEDGE-POWER

The project of relating and contrasting the *knowledge-power* of those who possess 'competency' of all kinds – cadres and managers, administrators and elite intellectuals, etc. – to the *property-power* of owners of capital is not self-evident. The nature of it is apt to shock common sense and the critical scholarly tradition, and raises a whole series of questions. Is this dichotomy, are these groupings, theoretically and empirically pertinent? What sociological and critical value can be ascribed to the notion of 'competent-elites'? What relation are we to establish between the two elements that make it up? And what is the relationship between knowledge and power? Does the concept of 'power', appended by turns to 'property' and to 'knowledge', present a substantial unity? And if so, what is it?

I attempt to answer these questions by reworking Foucault's conceptual framework, the aims of which are certainly not formulated in these terms but which nonetheless, it seems to me, help thus to broaden Marx's undertaking at the same time as call it into question. Foucault *identifies*, parallel to capital, *the other pole* of power and domination within modern society, that of power-knowledge (§2.1). He provides a proper *theorisation* of this pole, in which knowledge and power are articulated with each other (§2.2). And he provides a *critique* of it, which sets out both to supply weapons to counter its domination and to mobilise it for the goal of social emancipation (§2.3).

2.1 FOUCAULT EXPLORES THE 'POLE' THAT MARX LEFT IN A GREY ZONE

Based on what initially seemed a mere examination of the 'margins' of society, Foucault little by little uncovers *a different power* to that of capital. Thus sketched, this *different perspective*, which covers the entire social field, enters into competition with that bequeathed to us by the Marxist tradition (§2.1.1). Foucault permits us to recognise *this other pole* more effectively, a pole that is co-constitutive of the modern class structure and is not identified as such by Marx, who managed only to provide an historicist and thus erroneous concept of it (§2.1.2).

2.1.1 Foucault discerns knowledge-power alongside proprietor-power

Still close to the irruption of 1968, his lectures of 1972–73, *The Punitive Society,* present strong Marxist consonances. Attesting to this are certain lapidary expressions in the 'Summary' to this lecture series: says Foucault, liberal legislation at the end of the eighteenth century took as its aim 'a concentrated, diligent worker body, adjusted to the time of production, supplying the required force', and 'the prison-form of penalty corresponds to the wage-form of work' (*DE3*/468–9). Stéphane Legrand has highlighted the recurrence of a certain number of such statements throughout Foucault's course.[1] It is a matter, says Foucault, of a 'similar introduction of time into the system of capitalist power and into the system of penalty'.[2] The system of coercion is 'the political instrument of control and maintenance of relations of production'. The function of discipline is to 'subject the time of men's existence to this temporal system of the cycle of production'. In short, 'discipline' appears as a dimension of the relations of capitalist production: it is required, in some way prior to production, for the production of productive force.

Foucault, it will be noted, further adds to this in the series of talks he gave in Rio in 1973 (*EWF3*/1–89),[3] in which he designates the factory, prison, hospital, school, barracks, etc., as a set of institutions of 'sequestration'. 'What do this network and these institutions serve?' The reply is twofold. Their first function is to 'extract the maximum quantity of labour time' within the enterprise. 'Their second function consists in converting people's bodies into labour power. The function of transforming the body into labour power corresponds to

[1] Legrand, 'Le marxisme oublié de Foucault', in *Actuel Marx* No. 36, special issue *Marx et Foucault,* Paris: PUF, 2004.

[2] *La Société punitive*, Paris: Seuil/Gallimard, 2013 [73, 153, 216]. See also the lectures of 1973–74, *Psychiatric Power,* and in particular the parallel between the 'accumulation of men' and the 'accumulation of capital' (pp. 71–2).

[3] Here we are a stone's throw from the Chile of Allende, then burgeoning and impacting the entire South American intellectual Left.

the function of transforming time into labour time' (ibid., 82) … in view of 'the production and appropriation of capitalist hyperprofit' (ibid., 86). In sum, the said institutions are to be understood as functions of capitalist production.[4] Hyper-Marxism.

Legrand shows how, in *Discipline and Punish,* first published in 1975, Foucault renders Marxist concepts somewhat obsolete. The consequence, he says, is that an abstract concept of 'discipline' tends to prevail, which figures 'the fictive homology of different disciplinary institutions', connecting incomparable things with each other (school, prison …). Thus handled, 'discipline' would constitute a 'pseudo-concept'.[5] The Foucauldian analysis of the penitentiary, he argues, loses all its power if it is cut from its original and historically concrete reference within the constraints of capitalist production. It is certainly possible to argue in this fashion. But I would like for my part to put forward the idea that, seen from another angle, what Foucault here begins relative to the Marxist tradition is a

---

[4] Foucault thus mentions and seems to presume a set of hypotheses that are more or less particular or general: that the great confinement of the seventeenth century was a functional condition on the downward pressure on wages ('an extraordinarily elegant solution (…) a miracle remedy in the period of nascent capitalism' (*DE2*/298)); that the emergence of the prison in England was necessary for the protection of stocks (*EWF3*/69); and that a juridico-police order intensified in order to fix and control labour power, seize hold of workers' knowledge, 'epistemological power' (ibid., 83–4), and stigmatise a riot-bearing plebe ('Michel Foucault on Attica: An Inteview', 1974, in *Foucault Live,* pp. 113–21). This shows, in sum, the 'gigantic economic and political profit that the bourgeoisie draws from delinquency' (*DE2*/718–19).

[5] Legrand, 'Le marxisme oublié de Foucault'.

fecund redeployment that makes manifest a different power to 'capital' and apprehends it in its concrete texture, although at the most general level.

In this regard, moreover, we can find support in Legrand's analysis,[6] in which he shows how communication between the norms of one sphere and another is effected. In short, what the priest considered to be a sin, the judge a crime, the police delinquency, the pedagogue laziness, and the boss deficient labour power, the psychiatrist will interpret as a pathology. Corresponding to each of these versions of the norm is a type of disciplinary sanction but, in this, 'discipline' does not homogenise the field under a concept of 'coercive power'. Legrand is right. It is in each domain, he explains, that we must seek how a defined coding of the normal corresponds to a regime of subjectivity. Certainly. Yet Foucault does reveal a transversal factor here. When all is said and done, however, it is not *discipline*. It is, in my view, *knowledge-power*, which is heterogeneous in its content and its exercise, but identifiable as such in the diversity of its application of norms and disciplines. In his two lectures given in Turin in 1976 (see *PK*/78–108), Foucault defines his discovery by opposing himself to 'the economism of power' specific to Marxism: the analysis of power cannot be 'deduced from the economy' (p. 88). 'Recodification' manifests precisely the work of *a different* dominant power (*PK*/123): one that is not about economic *property*, but instead

---

[6] See his book *Les Normes chez Foucault*, Paris: PUF, 2007, notably pp. 81ff.

about *competency*. It manifests *the unity* of competency; it accomplishes the (class) complicity-competition between holders of power-knowledge. At least this is the interpretation I am putting forward.

In actual fact, Foucault introduces a new grid of analysis. He unveils discipline not as a simple functional requirement of the *capitalist order,* but also, next to the order of property and exchanges, as *another principle of order,* one pertaining to 'power-knowledge', which is also exercised throughout society in its entirety. Here he marks his essential 'structural' discovery. As emerges in the third part of the work titled 'Discipline', we are dealing here with *another sort of power* than that exercised by capitalists as such when they buy, sell means of production and products, hire and fire, make use of surplus product, decide to invest, to delocalise or to distribute dividends ... This other power pertains specifically to the possession and application of a recognised knowledge. It is indispensable for economic management, but is not limited to this sole use. As we see in the field of study to which Foucault has lent his name, it works via the panoptic organisation of space and time, via surveillance, examination, the elaboration of norms to enable hierarchisation and judgement, the definition of tasks, stages and modes of coordination ... Depending on the case, it tends toward production, correction and curing. It haunts the knowledge of the psychiatrist, the judge and the pedagogue. It subjects by separating, distinguishing, objectivising. This is knowledge that will become science. As Foucault puts it, 'The carceral network constituted one of the armatures [which thus also applies to the school and the hospital] of this power-knowledge that has made the human sciences historically possible. Knowable man (soul, individuality, consciousness, conduct, whatever it is called) is the object-effect of this analytical investment, of this domination-observation'.[7] This order is at once subjectivating and productive – two concepts, if truth be told, that remain for us to examine.

The prerogatives of knowledge-power, considered at the level of their daily exercise, seem rather feeble as compared with the property-power of high Finance, which may appear to dominate the world. But this is a phantom notion from which Foucault frees us: the modern form of society is not defined by the temporary configuration pertaining to neoliberalism. This form has to be deciphered in order to understand its metamorphoses. This will be seen below (§3.1.2) when I mark the difference in nature between these two dominant 'social forces', the hierarchisation and heterogeneity of the network of 'competency', and its porosity in relation to the whole of society. Its identification is a decisive preliminary moment on the path that leads to the recognition of what constitutes the potential of the 'fundamental class', or strength of the people.

The 'analogical table' presented above at §1.1.3 makes it possible to grasp the *structural* (sociological) signification of this grid of analysis. It brings to light the parallelism between the two constitutive poles of the 'modern form of society' – a concept that will be progressively defined throughout this

---

[7] Foucault, *Discipline and Punish,* p. 305.

investigation. In the language of Marx, the knowledge-power described here is no simple superstructural fact. It also has its base, which, as a site of production of utility, has to be seen as 'economic'. This is how Foucault will connect the emergence of the 'specific intellectual'[8] to the growing importance of the intellectual function as part of the development of 'technico-scientific structures'. He thus apprehends contemporary knowledge-power from its 'necessary base' (PK/122; tm), from the materiality of its inseparably technical and social 'apparatuses', which are *means* of producing, of making circulate, of consuming its *products* that are at once utilities – effects of health, of security, of education, et cetera – and facts of power. If this is right, both poles (market and organisation) are not distinguishable in the sense that one would be geared to production but not the other. We see this today in the fact that capital can very well seize hold of sectors (hospitals, schools, prisons, laboratories ...) that knowledge-power previously handled in non-market fashion as a public service, and give to the utilities produced the form of commodities and the function of profit. And if knowledge can provide power, this is due to the effects tied to the relation between actors and its specific material and social conditions of production. This is, at least, what may already be ventured at this still external,

---

8 See especially his admirable article 'The Political Function of the Intellectual', trans. Colin Gordon, published in *Radical Philosophy*, 16, 1977, pp. 12–14. (The French was published in *Politique-Hebdo* in 1976, reprinted in *DE3*/109–14, and is the summary of a longer interview first published in Italian.)

sociological level of analysis of 'knowledge' and 'power' and the 'productive' relations that obtain between them.

It remains for us to find out whether, by evoking this other general figure of 'power', Foucault opens up a problematic that is completely foreign to Marx's own. Is it possible to conceive a theoretical configuration that embraces both perspectives, and on the basis of which they are mutually able to shed light on and critique each other?

2.1.2 Why Marx's theory is missing a 'pole'

In my view, this critical inter-comprehension of 'Foucauldian-ism' and 'Marxism' – considered not as closed doctrines but as *research programmes* – implies a mutual re-elaboration of their concepts, enabling a theoretical re-founding that would generate a larger space into which both could be admitted. This is the aim of the approach I have termed metastructural, and which brings to light, it seems to me, precisely what it is that eludes Marx and motivates the recourse to Foucault.[9]

My point of departure is the idea, announced at the start of this work, that the modern social order has to be understood in terms of an 'instrumentalisation of *reason*'. If this is the case, the *dominant class* presents two poles, in accordance with the two '*rational* modes of coordination at the social level': market and organisation. Corresponding to these *two rational forms*

---

[9] The 'metastructural' approach mentioned in this paragraph is developed in *Théorie générale,* in *Explication et reconstruction du Capital,* and lastly in *L'État-monde.* The present work takes up this theoretical construction via an examination of the concepts of Foucault.

are *two social forces* (each one of which has its own mechanisms of reproduction): that of the *capitalists,* who dominate the market through the privileges of property, and that of the elites, who dominate organisation through the privileges of their 'competency', in the twofold sense of a *supposed knowledge that is doubled with a conferred authority.* Both social forces, that of property-power and that of knowledge-power, are simultaneously convergent and antagonistic, with a variability that depends on the circumstances. These go to making up the small few. Facing this oligarchy, the *fundamental or popular* class, which is the third social force – in reality, the first – is modulated in accordance with the diversity of links that its various 'fractions' (self-employed, private-sector wage earners, and public-sector wage earners) entertain with market processes and organisational processes, as well as with the mechanisms of exclusion to which the latter give rise. The definition of such concepts (notably those of 'competency', of 'competent-elites', of 'organisation' ...) and the concrete identification of such figures (who are the 'managers', the 'competent-elites' and so on?) is, of course, liable to raise many questions that I can work through only by pressing ahead with the account. The point here is only to state the guiding socio-historical line.

Let's note that this *dual* mode of coordination culminates not in the market (which gives its name to society: 'market society'), but in the supreme *organisation* that heads up the modern class structure: *the modern state institution.* This latter, by virtue of the 'metastructural priority' of the between-all over the between-each-person,[10] happens, regardless of the reality of the situation, to *align with* a democratic regime, at least starting from a determinate historical threshold. The modern state can *claim* to issue only from an organisation of speech presumed equal between all. Such is its *claim,* which is figured in the axiom 'one voice = one voice', and which is posited as the foundation of a common power. Concerning this modern fiction of a contractual-discursive order (which as we've seen Foucault constantly presumes in the background), we must try to elucidate its *ontological* status, i.e. its practical signification: a claim is not *nothing*.

If this is the case, if the dominant class comprises these two poles, then the Marxian approach to class structure is one-sided: Marx was indeed unable to grant 'organisation' its constitutive place in the modern form of society – in contrast with that he recognised the 'market' as having. Nor, therefore, was he able to grasp the place of 'competent-elites' as one social force within the dominant class. He studied diverse theoretical pairs: the productive/the unproductive, managers/subordinates, entrepreneurs/rentiers, etc. But he distributed these diverse figures around the opposition

---

[10] See *Théorie générale,* chapter 3, where I refer to a 'transcendental asymmetry' (in the sense of a historical transcendental specific to modernity) but which I now prefer to call a 'metastructural asymmetry'. Kant put forward this idea under the name of 'primitive communism': between persons that recognise each other as free and equal, no one can legitimately say 'this is mine', unless it is subject to an agreement among all on the rules concerning the use of the world. Such is the fictional presupposition of the state in modernity.

capitalist/wage earner. And he ignored the primary duo that the *'capitalists'* form together with the 'elites', which is specific to modern domination in that it is founded on the irreducible duality (market/organisation) of the 'instrumentalisation of reason'. More precisely, as he explains in the *Critique of the Gotha Programme*, looking beyond the passage to socialism, understood as concerted planning, he spied a further task: namely, that of doing away with the contradiction between what he designates as 'manual work' and as 'intellectual work' (let's translate it as 'knowledge-power'). But he left this task to those future times when 'abundance' would help resolve the problem. We have learnt from history that when the capitalists are chased out, there is a high risk of seeing the 'organisers' monopolise and concentrate power.

The paradox is that Marx is the one who identified the twofold structure of the 'instrumentalisation of reason' – constitutive of the modern social order – founded on an articulation of market and organisation.[11] He defined these latter, respectively, as an *a posteriori* order between independent producers and an *a priori* order in the framework of a unified power (the factory being *the* example). This conceptual pair market/organisation distinguishes two logics that in concrete reality are always closely combined.[12]

---

11 This is the hypothesis that I have tried to establish in my prior works.

12 Medicine, education, information, the distribution of mail, etc., depending on whether they are public or private, are propped up on different balances of market and organisation, but always contain both sorts of mediation at all levels: private medicine sells a market service on a health *market*, within the framework of a public *organisation* of diplomas,

In contrast with classical political economy, Marx put the theoretical question of socialism on the agenda, thus providing a historical perspective that has the articulation of market/organisation as its core.

Yet this is also the point at which his analysis fails. For the usage he makes of this duality is skewed, since for him it constitutes the principle of a *teleological* reading of modern history, whereby we proceed from the first term to the second, from market to organisation: the profound tendency of the *capitalist market* order – through the competitive processes of industrial concentration and the revolutionary opportunities that it offers to an increasingly numerous, educated and gathered proletariat – is, in his view, to evolve toward the possibility of a higher social order: a *concerted organisational* order, one organised between all people, called socialism. Marx thus uses the duality market/organisation in a *historical* but not a *structural* sense. However, precisely because this use is *historically erroneous,* it is also *structurally erroneous.* He was unable to see that it is both terms taken together, market and organisation, that define the *constitutive biopolarity* of modern class structure. This is why he failed to consider, *in its heterogeneity and in its materiality*, the structural correlate of property-power, which is to say *knowledge-power.*

---

competencies and possibly also of gradations of remuneration, and so on. All this is trivial. What is less so is to take up the theoretico-political challenges that this structural duality contains, according to the fluctuating line that separates 'governors' from the 'governed'.

It would fall to others, and notably to Foucault, to explore that 'other pole' of social space.[13] This feat was not accomplished in a systematic, encyclopaedic fashion, but its essential traits were revealed. However, we are yet to grasp what sort of unity it can be attributed and which relations it entertains with the pole of 'capital'. Both *mediations*, market and organisation, which structure this bipolar opposition, operate together as relays, as the continuation of discursive *immediation*, of cooperation founded directly on speech.[14] The *crucial point* of the 'instrumentalisation of reason' resides in the process whereby these 'mediations' are inverted into 'class factors' that subvert the discursive relation. Marx's failing was to portray socialism as a sort of triumph of democracy, of shared speech among all, that would have ensued from the abolition of the market and its opening on to 'concerted organisation'. We all know the turn of events such an attempt would take.

This gives us a preview of the socio-epistemic motifs and historico-political reasons for a meta-Marxist re-reading of Foucault, whose social and political critique is essentially devoted not to market capitalist domination, but to the power stemming from the 'other pole' of knowledge-power.

---

[13] This question in actual fact traverses, and notably since the 1930s, all the great sociologies, in which it is inflected in various ways. Thematics include: the era of managers, of bureaucratic society, of technostructure, Frankfurt School approaches, institutionalist approaches, approaches in terms of divisions between capital/*oikos*, entropy/organisation, economic capital and cultural capital, market 'sub-systems'/administration, etc.

[14] On this point see my *Etat-monde*, pp. 79–84: 'The historical, "discursive" hypothesis of modernity – Media, mediations and discursivity'.

2.2 FOUCAULT, THEORETICIAN OF THE
KNOWLEDGE-POWER OF 'COMPETENT-ELITES'

But which is the kind of knowledge at stake here? And which sort of power does it confer? From whom do these knowledges derive? From whom, these powers? These are the issues that this account seeks step by step to address. I attempt as a preliminary to define the Foucauldian project of a history of knowledge as a 'history of truth' (§2.2.1), contrast this theoretical programme with Marx's own (§2.2.2) and seek to address the conceptual framework in which these two ambitions can be related to one another (§2.2.3).

2.2.1 'The history of truth': the true,
the just and the authentic

Foucault, as an admirer of Koyré (*DE1*/170), began his research in a period of philosophical effervescence surrounding the history of the sciences. But with *The History of Madness in the Classical Age* he set out, in the spirit of the periodical *Annales*, to walk the path of a history that is no longer 'internal' but 'external' (*EWF3*/4), a *social* history of knowledge, which he deciphers on the basis of an examination of the periodic renewal of domains of objects, types of knowledge, statuses of actors or of subjects concerned, material techniques and apparatuses, strategies of diverse groups, and also, in *The Order of Things*, on the basis of epistemic transformations affecting the ensemble of forms of knowledge. This is how 'truths' come to succeed one another, truths that are generally accepted and have authority. It is well known that Foucault acknowledged, in this regard, the significant impetus he received from Canguilhem (in the wake of Bachelard), a theoretician of discontinuity, the transformation of epistemological fields and the use of concepts.[15] But Foucault came gradually to take on a vaster project, identified *après coup* as a 'history of truth'. 'My problem', he later wrote, 'was, in relation to madness, to know how one was able to have the discourse on madness operate in the sense of discourses of truth, that is to say, discourses with the status and function of true discourse. In the West, this is scientific discourse. This is the sense in which I wanted to tackle sexuality' (*DE3*/312).

Beginning in the 1970s, Foucault sees 'knowledge' and 'power' as interfering in each other more explicitly. 'Each society', he says, 'has its regime of truth, its general politics of truth: that is to say, the type of discourse that it accepts and makes function as true; the mechanisms and authorities that enable one to distinguish true and false statements, the means by which each is sanctioned; the techniques and procedures accorded value in the acquisition of truth; the status of those who are charged with saying what counts as true'. That is, 'a political economy of truth' (*PK*/131).

The *positive* character thus tied to the object of his research under the sign of 'truth' contrasts sharply with the perspectives

---

15 See Judith Revel, *Foucault, une pensée du discontinu,* Paris: Fayard, 2010, pp. 47–55. But the heritage adopted is also Braudel's, as Jean-François Bert underscores in his *Introduction à Michel Foucault,* Paris: La Decouverte, 2011, p. 19.

inspired by Marx, whom Foucault regularly reproaches for having remained wedded, in examining the same phenomena, to the viewpoint of 'ideology', when not to the progress of science or to the 'productive forces'.[16] In effect everything transpires as if both a 'history of truth' and a 'history of ideology' came face to face and became entangled around the relation they entertain with power. Let's try to untangle this maze. And for starters grasp where things are with the 'truth' here in question.

A claim of validity, Geltungsanspruch

This 'history of truth' does not concern truth as such, but the history of what is held to be true.[17] It thus takes as its proper object *claims* to truth and its *recognition,* which are related to the technical and institutional conditions of their reproduction. Following Wittgenstein and Austin, it is therefore legitimate, it seems to me, to consider them in terms of *speech acts*: as *claims* involved in intersubjective practices, inscribed in 'apparatuses'. We are dealing here with statements that lay

---

[16] See (*PK*/118) his refusal of approaches that go via 'ideology', insofar as they present an obstacle to understanding how 'effects are truth are produced within discourse that in themselves are neither true nor false'.

[17] This is what explains Jacques Bouveresse's reluctance to use the term 'truth' (see Didier Eribon (ed.) *L'Infréquentable Michel Foucault,* Paris: EPEL, 2001, pp. 136ff). Yet the Foucauldian concept of 'truth' is to be understood in an entirely different sense. See Thomas Boccon-Gibod, *Michel Foucault, dire la vérité,* Poitiers: Sceren CDNP, 2013. 'Whereas truth is commonly understood as a quality of what is said, Foucault', he writes, 'introduces [...] a radically new perspective: the truth of saying in its relation to the life of the one who states it.' This is also the sense in which I talk about a 'claim to truth'.

claim to communication, in the Habermasian sense.[18] If things proceed in this way, the 'truth' Foucault speaks of never occurs on its own: its discourse necessarily bears the other two dimensions constitutive of any such speech act. Its claim has to be understood in its triple content of *validity*. This 'discourse of truth' does not only claim to be *true*. It also presents itself as *just*, that is, as falling within the 'normality' that it prescribes. And it appeals to the *authentic*, that is, to a truth pertaining to the subjects who proclaim themselves in this discourse.[19] It is the site of an instrumentalisation of reason. But one cannot reduce it to the *effects* it produces on interlocutors. We are dealing here with presuppositions that are objectively present in discursive apparatuses – both institutional and material – through which actors come face to face in 'games of truth', in

[18] The idea is very simple: when the lift operator says 'it is prohibited to smoke', he enters into the triple claim of the *true* (it is unwholesome), the *just* (it is incorrect here) and the *authentic* (I am justified in reminding you). For a comprehensive analysis, see Jurgen Habermas, *The Theory of Communicative Action*, Vol. 1, trans. Thomas McCarthy, Boston: Beacon Press, 1984. The claim to validity thus comprises three components: a claim to truth-efficacy (*Wahrheit-Wirksamkeit*), one to justice (*Richtigkeit*) and one to authenticity (*Wahrhaftigkeit*). See the table presented on page 439 of Habermas's *Theorie des kommunikativen Handelns*, Frankfurt am Main: Suhrkamp, 1985.

[19] Thus understood, 'communicative action' is oriented around a common definition of the situation in view of a *consensual organisation* of each individual's plans. In the Habermasian perspective, at issue is to determine under which conditions communication is able to establish itself as the effective norm of social life. While I refer to this concept, my goal is entirely different. I take a non-normative but instead analytical perspective that runs counter to the political, historical and social theory put forward by Habermas, which I deploy in order to define the nature of the *claim* inherent to the *presupposition posited* by the modern class structure and therefore also by modern class struggle. See my *Théorie générale*, pp. 412–26 and *L'État-monde*, pp. 74–92.

manoeuvres of instrumentalisation and of emancipation, thus producing themselves as determinate subjectivities. Foucault's 'truths' are to be understood according to this triple register.

1. *The efficacy of truth.* 'The history of truth' is given as a 'history of veridiction', of the diction of the *true.* In the modern era this supposed truth is that of science. Foucault follows it through diverse registers: the history of madness, of sexuality and so on. In *Discipline and Punish,* this truth is that of the discourses and practices of the prison, the asylum, etc., which claims to correct, cure, educate. In the lectures of 1977–79, the specificity of liberal governmentality is cast as residing in the way it allows natural laws, declared to have been scientifically established, to play out freely.

2. *The justice of the norm.* Foucault insists on the fact that the *norm* tends to replace *right,* or rather to 'mingle' with it. Beccaria's 'legalist theory' provides an allegedly exemplary version of this progression – the issue being to repair a wrong inflicted on society – to a problematic of 'control' and 'surveillance', on the basis notably of the impetus supplied by Bentham's panoptic utopia (*EWF3*/70ff.). This 'mixture' is well expressed in the broad concept of 'justice' (*Richtigkeit* in German) pertaining to a 'social world' in which norms and values, interests and ethics intertwine. This new power, manifest in *the rise of the norm,* is that of a *new* world of *competent-elites,* who are placed in charge of bodies and souls, of just ends and adapted means. They have the competency enabling them to discern those that the law is unable to: abnormal persons, deviants, the ill, etc. As the ill come to replace criminals, 'the effects of truth of a science are

at the same time effects of power' (*FL*/198). The titulars of this truth, claimed to be that of a science, exercise a normative function in the place of the men of law. They say what it is *just* to do. Similarly with the hygienist doctors, who prescribed a bright and transparent urban design (*FL*/229), and so on. The power of competency, which thus impregnates all society, is exercised in the name of the norm, which is irreducible to the truth of science. It states, at the same time as that which is true, that which is 'normal'.[20] One of the most important heritages of Foucault's research in this regard is to be sought in a Foucauldian sociology that designates the norm as the operator of a new 'bureaucratisation of the world'.[21]

3. *Authenticity and authority of discourse.* The (claim to) truth that Foucault speaks about gets affirmed only insofar as it is shared: not only recognised but effectively ratified by a subject that itself enters into interlocution. And that therefore *confesses*. 'What I mean by confession', Foucault says, 'is all those procedures by which the subject is incited to produce a discourse of truth about his sexuality which is capable of having effects on the subject himself'.[22] Sexuality is called to

---

[20] In *De Canguilhem à Foucault: la force des norms* (Paris: Fabrique, 2009), Pierre Macherey shows notably how these authors provide the notion of norm with a dynamic meaning, one that pertains to an inventive process triggered by the emergence of new problems and that transforms the field of experience.

[21] See Béatrice Hibou's *La Bureaucratisation du monde à l'ère néolibérale*, Paris: La Découverte, 2013. It deals with what is today an immense field of research.

[22] *PK*/216. (Modern) novelty emerges when 'people are told that the secret of their truth lies in the region of their sex' (214).

state itself in propositions that are (true, just and) *authentic*: by confessing, the subject declares as *his* the discourse of 'sexual science'. Similarly in the orders of misdemeanour, health, education. If things proceed in this way, it is not as regards a corrected, cured or educated subject, but insofar as the subject *recognises itself* in this power of correction, cure or instruction. In this sense, this claim emerges in inter-interpellation, which posits the individual as subject, the interpellator as much as the interpellated.[23] This is not to say that this game of truth remains enclosed in a space of singular subjects tied in micro-relations. The truth is 'produced and transmitted under the control, dominant if not exclusive, of a few great political and economic apparatuses (university, army, writing, media)' and it is the 'stake of a whole political debate and social confrontation (ideological struggles)' (*PK*/131–2).[24] In other terms, 'truth' only generates its product-effects by means

---

[23] The confession is demanded 'in justice, medicine, education, family relationships, and love relations [...]' (*HS*/59). There is a supposed innocence in saying it all, or in showing it all. The reader will not fail to observe the relation between the demand to 'tell everything', which is repeated continuously (*HS*/21) by experts in charge of souls and bodies, from confessors to psychiatrists, and the modern claim to govern oneself under a regime of speech (in which one person = one voice) and to resolve public matters inside the presumed authority that ensues from it, that of public and transparent speech.

[24] See also chapter 3 of the *History of Sexuality*, Vol. 1, 'Scientia sexualis': 'The confession is a ritual of discourse in which the speaking subject is also the subject of the statement; it is also a ritual that unfolds within a power relationship, for one does not confess without the presence (or virtual presence) of a partner who is not simply the interlocutor but the authority who requires the confession, prescribes and appreciates it, and intervenes in order to judge, punish, forgive, console and reconcile [...]', pp. 61–2.

of technico-organisational apparatuses of production. The properly *modern* character of 'truth' resides in its reference not only to science and technical efficacy, but also, correlatively, to its public character. In contrast with ancient erotic techniques, Foucault stresses, the modern discourse of sex – and this also applies to the other 'discourses of truth' – pertains to *public* space. This is the sense in which we can understand the recurrent theme of 'statification' or 'governmentalisation' of knowledge-power (medicine, school, justice, army).[25] Here, it seems to me, is the truth, metastructurally modern, of this 'discourse of truth': it implies a correlation between a public-state discourse and the discourse of subjects that make it theirs, according to the presupposition that *supposedly* inscribes all of life in this regime of 'speech'.[26]

The Foucauldian project, as we see, *circumvents the history of sciences* in that it does not deal with the progressive conquest of what we can see today has 'scientific' value, but describes the trajectory of what is given and practised as truth in relation to the effects of power, domination, life and subjectivation attached to it. He *goes beyond a mere history of ideas* in that he inserts scientific discourses into practices, and then these practices into apparatuses. I have aimed to show that in the material, ontologico-social framework he

---

25 On modern 'sexual science', the object of 'truth' of argued public discourse, in contrast with ancient and oriental 'erotics', private wisdoms linking disciples to masters, see *The History of Sexuality,* Vol. 1, pp. 53–73. On the statification of the biological, see *Society Must Be Defended,* pp. 239–40.

26 On this concept of 'regime of speech', see my *L'Etat-monde,* pp. 84–7.

brings to light, *truths, norms* and *subjects* are all simultaneously at work.

These are not, as is well known, the terms in which Foucault states his discourse. But, it seems to me, this is all fully implied in his approach. However, to avoid misunderstandings, I would like to indicate in advance the direction in which this reading will take us. This triple invocation of reason-rationality, inherent to the 'claim of validity', never appears from 'above' except as instrumentalised by powers that are concerned not only with making statements but with their own effective exercise in the social conditions of that enunciation, that is to say in a 'class' context. But, if we bear in mind that power is not to be understood as a simple *transitive* model *dominant/dominated*, but as a reciprocal *relation,* a clash of powers (of ascendency on social things and on oneself), one comes to see that this positivity, this historical creativity immanent to the process of properly modern domination, resides in the fact that top-down power encounters a living force from below, which is itself configured, on this side of instrumentalisation, by its social relation to this common, 'bipolar' reason-rationality, its relation to a common potential of 'mediation' as well as of discourse. The productivity of power is not a simple fact that descends from on high. That is what – in a shortcut that might still appear cloudy – I shall try to establish.

In Foucault's research between 1971 and 1976, this 'history of truth' concerns not *property*, but what I designate as the 'other class factor', namely *competency*: this is the capacity, of which the competent-elites are the titulars, to be recognised (and to establish oneself) as a bearer of 'truth'– a truth that combines the true, the just and the authentic. With this, the hypothesis that there is a parallelism between both 'poles' of the modern social order respectively recognised by Marx and by Foucault starts to take on consistency. The continuing problem, however, is that these two theoretical components seem very heterogeneous and that each has its own historicity: the history of 'truth' is not that of 'capital'. Before tackling this crucial question, we must nonetheless account for another difficulty, which arises on account of the change of object and register that we observe in Foucault toward the end of the 1970s.

2.2.2 The truths of government

1. With the lectures of 1977–79, the horizon effectively changes. The focus no longer bears on the practices of *competent-elites* in their domain of competency, but instead on practices of 'government', and of government by means of 'political economy', which might at first seem rather to be the business of capitalists. This truth is that of the 'governors'. The existence of this collective actor is born only through its correlation with the collective of the 'governed', in a specific representation of the social *whole* that clearly resolves for an officially *nominalist* programme. Who governs then? For whom are these 'truths of government'? Let us again revisit this notion of 'truth', but this time as it appears in the field of 'government by means of political economy' as well as in its relation to the 'critique of the political economy' put forward

by Marx. How are we to assess these 'truths of government'? What is the status of this discourse in which 'civil society' becomes a point of reference?

2. Foucault urges us to take the categories of 'civil society' as 'transactional realities' (*réalités de transaction*). 'I believe', he writes, 'that we must be very cautious as to the degree of reality that we grant this civil society.' It is not to be taken as a 'primary and immediate' reality standing opposite political institutions. 'It is something that forms part of modern governmental technology. (...) That does not mean that it has no reality. Civil society is like madness and sexuality, what I call transactional realities, that is to say, it is in the interplay precisely of relations of power and of everything that eludes them – it is this from which is born, as it were, at the interface of the governors and the governed, those transactional and transitory figures that, although they have not always existed, are no less real for all that.' (*BB*/297; tm). This transactional reality between actors, this pragmatic reality of inter-discourse – such is to my mind the strongest interpretation of 'government by means of political economy' – is not the *real of (class) structure* in the society under consideration; it does not define a pure objectivity. Nor is it an *ideal* to bring forth. It is the transactional reality of a real order of statements bound up in real practices, that of the practical presuppositions inherent to a determinate social structure. It emerges in the form of a *historical a priori* that is to be understood in its own 'materiality'. In the field on which Foucault crosses Marx, it relates to what I have designated as the '*metastructure*'.

3. Precisely such a 'transactional reality' is in fact formulated in the analytical account in Section 1 of Book 1 of *Capital.* Here Marx very precisely describes the logic of the 'civil society' about which liberals speak. He defines modern society as a 'market society' and does so prior even, in the development of the account, to his qualification of its capitalist character. He views the social logic of market production as the presupposition of capitalism, as its stated logic. The first chapter uncovers its *rationality,* its *Wahrheit* (the configuration of competition, based on private property, maximises the production of use-values and optimises the allocation of factors) and its *legitimacy,* its *Richtigkeit* (which knows only of free and equal partners). To reprise the above-analysed formulations of Foucault (§1.2.3), Marx shows how the juridical comes to be 'indexed' to the economic, and vice versa, in an economic/juridico-political (meta)structuration inside the very core of the concept of market production. The second chapter of *Capital* considers the third demand involved in the transaction of communication: that of the *identity* of the citizen who claims and of the *authenticity* of his governmental claim. Marx shows that as money and the market form[27] of which it is the condition are not facts of nature – since history has produced other sorts of arrangement – they thus imply a 'social act' that posits them, that proclaims some such social

---

[27] Part of a linguistic usage that Marxism inherited from Hegel, the term 'form' refers simply to all types of social construction, whether at issue is the market or capital, the metastructure or the structure, the wage relation or the state. It does not harbour any theoretical 'secret' within it.

order. 'In the beginning was the deed,' he wrote[28]: this is not a historical beginning, but a *principle of this particular social logic*, which is being continuously reinstituted. Such an act between supposedly *free* market-producers can only be a *pact*, in which is affirmed the freedom of all under the law of the market. It is an act of language in the sense of the Johannic archive: 'in the beginning was the Word'. It nonetheless pertains not to an ahistorical transcendental ontology, but to a historically determined social configuration, for which they will have to account.

4. So Marx is further required to establish the conditions of this third term: *How do the actors who hold this discourse as their truth, who hold themselves to be the authentic subjects of that 'truth', arise?* Beyond the internal critique of that claim, which is stated in that Section 1 (in the famous paragraph devoted to 'commodity fetishism'),[29] Marx in actual fact

---

[28] See *Capital,* Vol. 1, chapter 2, p. 180. It is remarkable that this passage is regularly ignored by philosophical commentary on this work. It poses a problem that a certain doxa, failing to understand that we are dealing with a properly metastructural position, is unable to work through. For a reading of these first two chapters, I take the liberty of referring to my *Explication et reconstruction du Capital,* pp. 45–91. In it, I show how Marx rewrites Hobbes's pact in the apocalyptic terms of alienation.

[29] It is a matter of a twofold critique, first a phenomenological one of commodity fetishism in chapter 1, then an ontological-critical one of the 'social act' that institutes the market in chapter 2 – an 'ontology of the act'. This second stage, strangely ignored, is indeed that which governs the first: only the extent to which society functions effectively under the blow of this *act* that *institutes* the law of the market – that is to say, as soon as producers-citizens allow themselves to be dispossessed of their ability to organise among themselves according to 'concerted planning' – do social relationships come to appear as things.

seeks to establish the nature of the historically determined *real-structural* process that *generates* this market apparatus in its generalised form, inscribing all subjectivities within it. He shows, in Section 3, how, via the capitalist mechanism of wage exploitation that turns labour power itself into a commodity, the market is accomplished as *universal* rule. This inaugural 'act' comes to be *posited,* or produced, in the *structural* fact of capitalism as its *metastructural* presupposition. 'Capital' is the structure that generates the 'market' metastructure as its universal presupposition. It posits it as a 'transactional reality' through which actors *communicate in their practices:* as a fiction according to which the wage relation, being a market relation, is held to be rational (truth), equal (justice) and free (authenticity) – a fiction in which the wage earner participates as a free partner. The *reality* of this fiction resides in the (contradictory) effects that it generates in class confrontation.[30] The force of Marx's *dialectical* analysis thus resides in its tackling head-on the question of knowing which *social structure* is required for the development of *practices* that posit this *metastructure* as their presupposition, that posit such claims, 'truths', statements, as those of civil society, taken in the Foucauldian sense as a 'transactional reality'.

From Section 1 to Section 3 of Book 1, Marx proceeds from the study of 'liberalism' (understood as the 'discourse'

---

30 We will return to this at §4.1.1 concerning the 'political contradiction of capitalism'.

of capitalists identifying with the universal discourse of partners in a market) to that of capitalism'.[31] He takes us from 'civil society' to 'class society'. He takes us from the *abstract* moment of the account in which the juridical comes to be 'indexed' to the economy – to an economy fictively defined by relations of market production – to the more *concrete*, that is to say conceptually more *'determined'*, form, which is that of capitalism,[32] the latter being 'determined' through the identification of labour force itself as commodity. And at issue, in this second moment, is a wholly other reality, a *structural* one, able to be understood only in relation to the first *metastructural* reality, and on the *basis of it,* as the order

---

[31] The term 'liberalism' has, as is well known, several meanings. Foucault intends it in the eighteenth-century sense, which asserts the rational primacy of the market without excluding certain forms of organisation. The 'liberalisms' that later arise in various places are distinguished from one another by the respective weight they grant to each of the mediations; the claim they share is that their economic equation is of a piece with 'political liberalism'. For my part, I propose to break with these termi-nologies. By 'liberalism' I mean the perspective specific to individuals with privileges of capital (for whom, by nature, 'the world is a *market*'). 'Socialism' is henceforth the perspective proper to those with privileges of competency, in the sense of knowledge-power (which leads to the triumph of organisation under the form of 'real socialism' when they succeed in monopolising power). 'Communism' is therefore the perspective open to those who possess no *privileged* hold over either one of these 'mediations', of which they are nonetheless part, insofar as the mediations pertain to their own social reason, common to all.

[32] In Marx's epistemology, the opposition *abstract/concrete* indicates a difference in the degree of determination: the account proceeds from the most 'general' to the most 'determinate'. When the analysis comes to show that the former moment is the posited presupposition of the latter, it discovers the dialectical relationship between both these terms.

of the account taken in *Capital* attests.[33] And here we can invoke Deleuze: 'The universal [...] explains nothing; it is the universal that needs to be explained.'[34]

5. The analytic step, which goes from liberalism (understood as the subjective discourse of capitalists) to capitalism, is not one that Foucault takes. In the lectures of 1977–79, he remains within the *discourse* of liberalism – in this indetermination that the following significant statement may justify: 'I have never written anything but fictions' (*FL*/213). Truth to tell, he *relates* a fiction, but without taking up, in contrast with Marx, the question of its status as reality and the conditions of its production. He does not analyse capitalist *practices*. He indeed presumes that the unfortunate realities of capitalism exist in the background, and often brings this out eloquently with his sensitive prose. He does not revisit the Marxian economic analysis of exploitation, whether to criticise it or to correct it. He changes scene: from class practices to practices of government. He doubtless does not forget that government is a matter *of class*. But his object of study is governmental technologies as such, the 'politics' of *state*. He does not see them as pertaining to a politics of capital (as

---

33 Once more, the concept of metastructure – which is the posited presupposition of the structure, in the sense that, in *Capital,* Section 1 presents the presupposition posited by Section 3 – is not to be confounded with that of superstructure.

34 Gilles Deleuze, 'What is a *dispositif*?' in *Michel Foucault, Philosopher,* trans. Timothy J. Armstrong, New York: Harvester Wheatsheaf, 1992, p. 162.

happens rather one-sidedly in a certain Marxism). He expresses them in the discourse of the actors themselves, in *their* discourse of 'truth'. He connects them to practices included in 'apparatuses', but without linking them to the 'structure', which is what Marx does in passing – between Section 1 and Section 3 – from the market to capital. He remains in a context of 'transactional realities', wherein socio-economic relations are considered in terms of exchange relations in a market, whose productivity must be optimised by allowing its natural game to run.

6. If we are to conclude, it is necessary to consider more broadly the tableau that Foucault proposes of the liberal era. If one actually pulls back a little with respect to his guiding statements, it becomes evident that he presents us with another 'truth of government'. While he seems to be entirely bound up in the self-evidence of a market order, which he designates as that of the 'economy', in actual fact what he presents to us is a *governmental rationality with two poles.* The classical liberalism he describes to us – in contrast with the neoliberalism to which he subsequently comes – in fact never ceases, despite its reference to the market as a 'natural order', to consider state 'interventions' as indispensible. The splendid tableau we are given of disciplinary institutions (hospitals, schools, infrastructures, royal manufacturers, etc.) bears witness to the fact that intervention, far from being the exception, is part of the rule. It is not simply a matter of interventions in the market: *it is a matter of an economy* (producing use-values), an economy that is organised in parallel and in co-imbrication with the

market economy. Even if his stated aims are not explicit about this, the governmental truth of 'liberalism' of which Foucault speaks, a corollary of the liberal subject, articulates both orders of reason-rationality, one market, the other organisational.[35]

My argument is that the prevalence of the former over the latter defines the historical phase of liberal or bourgeois hegemony. At bottom, this is exactly Foucault's conception of things as well. Let's note that he actually examines liberalism not as a total novelty, figuring the spirit of the rationality of an era, but as a historical reversal, as a change of equilibrium, as a reaction *that comes to limit, to counterbalance, preceding technologies: those of* state reason, which conforms to *Polizeiwissenschaft*, and those, older still, of *sovereignty*. This is a change in the regime of 'hegemony': a concept of this sort does in fact come to have a place in Foucault's work.[36] It remains to us to formulate a theory of hegemony in modern times that would enable an assessment of the successive *hegemonic* truths and their historical conditions of emergence – including the future developments to be expected.

---

35 In this 'metastructural grid', to repeat, reason and rationality comprise the two 'faces', and market and organisation the two 'poles'. See note 7 of the Introduction.

36 See *PK/*156, in 'The eye of Power', an interview conducted with J. P. Barou and M. Perrot in 1977. The proximity between the approach in terms of 'government', that is, of the 'conduct of conducts', *versus* violence or contract, and the Gramscian conception of 'hegemony' is highlighted by Thomas Lemke. See 'Marx sans', in *Actuel Marx,* No. 36, *Marx et Foucault,* Paris: PUF, 2004.

This is not the direct topic of the present research.[37] But we can already represent these 'truths' as referring to two diametrically opposed *social forces* that are (unequally) able to enforce their 'government', in the active sense that Foucault gives this term. A theory of hegemony has to enable an analysis of the historical course of their relations, and of their basic class relationships (themselves active stakeholders in both 'mediations', the market and organisation), the length of a history to be understood also in 'systemic' terms, in the sense of the world-system. But to take a clearer look at the issue, we have still to consider more closely the relation between the concepts that Foucault develops and the structural matrix advanced by Marx.

2.2.3 Refounding the Marxian project to admit Foucault

No one will be surprised that I am embarking on a Marxian admission of Foucault and a Foucauldian admission of Marx on the basis of concepts that are apparently foreign to them, such as those of 'poles', 'organisation' and 'competency'. If I proceed in this way it is because such an undertaking can only be accomplished by ascending higher in the conceptual chain, by rediscovering the point at which their projects distinguish themselves from one another, which is also the point we must

---

[37] The second part of *Le Néolibéralisme, Un autre grand récit*, Paris: Les Prairies Ordinaires, 2016, entitled 'Le néolibéralisme dans la séquence des temps modernes', is devoted to the formulation of a 'metastructural' theory of hegemony.

return to in order to have them encounter and confront one another anew.

In this regard, two orders of preliminary clarification are required. On the one hand, it is a matter of the relation *between the two poles* of property-power and of knowledge-power within the dominant class, and, on the other hand, of *relations within the pole of knowledge-power*, which are stamped by tension between the terms 'power' and 'knowledge', and that we find in analogical fashion in the designation 'competent-elites'.

1. The relationship between both poles as sites of power

To maintain that the issue here has to do with two poles of modern domination means that these latter are in some way *comparable in terms of power*: of the struggle for power, of the division of power, etc. Required here is a common concept of 'power', one that makes it possible to conceive privileges of such different natures as property and competency as being *privileges of power.*

In what way does the ownership of capital constitute a power? It may seem that what surplus-value makes it possible to accumulate is *wealth.* For what first comes within the property of the capitalist entrepreneur – a figure of reference in Marx's account – is a *set of commodities,* the value of which is higher than that required as investment in wages and means of production. As soon as the sale is accomplished, the appropriate surplus takes the form of abstract wealth, which constitutes a power: *proprietor-power.* The power to dispose of it arbitrarily, to use it to purchase luxury goods, means of production and labour power (in contrast with feudal wealth, which Foucault analyses as the 'means by which both violence and the law were brought to bear on the life and the death of others'. *EWF3/41*). Or else, to use it for purely speculative purposes. The classical economists maintained that property is power. The distinction to be made here is between the 'power' a wage gives, which is to buy subsistence goods, and that conferred by capitalist property, which is power over other people and over the means to set them to work with a view to making a profit out of them, as well as to influence, in alliance with others, the legislature, the executive, the judiciary etc. In short, accumulated surplus-value is property as social power, which in the last resort is verifiable in the purchase of labour power with a view to its own accumulation.

What is the story with the other pole? Knowledge-power also constitutes a power over things and persons, and is exercised by individuals by virtue of their place in an organisation (enterprise, administration, profession, army, city, state) and with reference to the social recognition that grants them competency. In the exercise of a determinate function, one exercises a particular sort of power: managerial power over workers, medical power over the ill, university power over students, etc. This power also extends, of course, to the material and symbolic apparatuses involved in these functions. It is produced, reproduced and accumulated, is gained and lost, according to other mechanisms than those of property, and which are sociologically identifiable. Attached to it are different social satisfactions. But the issue in both cases is a faculty to 'have the other at one's disposal', within forms and limits that are defined in each instance (and in both cases it remains for us to clarify the concerns of holism and nominalism respectively attributed to Marx and to Foucault).

Property-power and knowledge-power, insofar as they proceed from 'two primary forms of rationality at the social scale', are evidently endowed with some form of productivity. This is why they are instrumentalised, but this productivity is never cancelled out in instrumentalisation (as Foucault says, if the issue was only one of repression, do you think that they would have ever been accepted?). These are distinct powers, but they are not incomparable. That is why they can both, or by turns, coordinate and clash with each other. The question of *hegemony* will be precisely that of the balance between these two sorts of powers, which are always closely involved with one another and exercised by individuals *competing* against one another on the market or within a form of organisation. Both powers are notably combined at the summit due to the fact that top managers share in capitalist profits (which may take the form of high salaries), and that large-scale capitalists participate in management. And, more generally, because the market and organisation are always mixed up with one another. Each of these two functions nonetheless refers to a different logic of power.

In this regard, the standard Marxism of philosophers-interpreters in general remains blocked by a curious 'epistemological-obstacle', in some sense constructed by Marx himself through the duality 'formal subsumption'/'real subsumption'.[38] After a first phase of purely 'formal' subsumption of work by capital, that of the family capitalist production in the countryside, or even in manufacturing, where signs of the craft industry survive, then comes 'real' subsumption, which organises space and time, the body and mind of the worker under the total hold of 'capital'. It was necessary, of course, to name this passage to a more organised-disciplined form, which progressively neutralises the producer's hold on the means of production, a process that began in the industrial factory and is continued through Taylorism (where the worker's knowledge is seized as well), then Fordism, Toyotism, up until neoliberal totalitarian management.[39] But this recourse to the philosophical register – *formal/real* – is misleading here. *In actual fact* the hold of what is called 'capital' is *genuinely* exercised from the beginning. And what, in its most developed forms, is called the 'real subsumption *of capital*' is a modality of power that can be discovered just as easily in *non-capitalist* sectors (prison, hospital, school, administration in general) and in 'real socialism' (that is, state socialism, from the enterprise to the gulag) – in a wholly other context, then, than that of 'capital'. The duality formal/real therefore generates a pseudo-concept. It *occults* what Foucault had precisely brought to light: the fact that modernity presents

---

[38] See the account in the appendix to *Capital*, Book 1, titled 'Results of the Immediate Process of Production', pp. 948–1,084.

[39] From a metastructural perspective, I revisit the question of the effects of management on subjectivation in chapter 6 of *Le Néolibéralisme, Un autre grand récit*, Paris: Les Prairies Ordinaires, 2016, entitled 'Les sujets du néolibéralisme'.

another mechanism of power, another 'pole' of instrumentalised reason, which is not that of the market instrumentalised as capital, but which itself traverses the entire society, including in its non-capitalist components. In short, the modern form of society is to be understood as a co-imbrication between market and *organisation,* both instrumentalised as class factors. In this way, the tasks of analysis and critique broaden, as do those of class struggle: they must be led on two fronts. They must be undertaken not against 'capital' but against a two-headed hydra: against the masters of the market *and against the potentates of organisation.* This is precisely where Foucault's critique of Marxism effectively intervenes and his 'discovery' appears as an essential recourse for thinking through a more general problematic of emancipation.

2. The tension between 'competency' and 'management' within the pole of knowledge-power

The Foucauldian investigation here is particularly fecund insofar as it furnishes, in the terms of 'knowledge-power', a concept that is suited to this 'other pole'. But is it necessary to designate it as a pole of 'organisation' or even of 'elite-competency'?

Why '*competency*'? This term in effect befits the 'power' it brings to light along with that attached to *capitalist property.* 'Competency', as we have seen, is to be understood here in the double sense of the term: *a supposed knowledge* and *a power (authority) conferred* by a social body that is itself endowed with competence, that is to say, whose authority is recognised. Foucault speaks in this sense about 'established power', one that 'enables and assures the exercise of a power' (*SPu*/237). The 'privileges of competency' are opposed in this sense to the 'privileges of property'. To speak, as Bourdieu does, of 'cultural capital' and of the cultural 'arbitrariness' that goes hand in hand with it is one way of thematising the 'instrumentalisation of reason'.[40] Foucault moves in the same register when he deciphers a Janus-face-type 'knowledge-power', a power of life and a power of subjectivation – depending on whether understanding-reason is or is not reversed and made into a class factor within the confrontation of a class relationship. So, if having employed the expression 'elites-and-experts' for a long time,[41] I now prefer the syntagm 'competent-elites', this is in

---

[40] Bourdieu also situates himself on the critical terrain where knowledge-competency of acquired and dispensed forms of knowledge overlaps with the power-competency of received and exercised authority. He is interested, similarly to Foucault, in its exercise, but also, in contrast to the latter, in the conditions of its reproduction, which is seen as having a class structure. Foucault's lack of interest in that aspect of things is rather troubling. In order to conceive the reproduction of a class privilege, it is necessary to think in terms of structure. But, as we shall see below, Foucault finds this kind of conceptuality repugnant.

[41] This is the formulation used in *Altermarxisme,* which I wrote together with Gérard Duménil. Duménil, notably in his collaborative work with Dominique Levy, uses the term 'cadres'. He considers that the cadres form an intermediary class that, on the condition of forming an alliance with the 'popular classes', is apt to reach a form of hegemony that would sweep aside the capitalist class. This approach – let's call it 'cadrist' – and the metastructural approach notably share their discerning of three primary social forces, considered as essential points of reference for a periodisation of modern hegemony and for a political strategy of emancipation. Whereas the former approach speaks of a 'class' of cadres, the latter speak of a 'pole' of leaders-experts among the dominant or privileged class. For more on the affinities and differences between them, see *Altermarxisme,* pp. 151–2.

order to account better for the relation of immanence between both terms, which is expressed in the term 'knowledge-power' or 'power-knowledge': whether at issue is production and administration, the management of bodies or the directing of minds and souls, it is always a matter of the privilege of 'directing' others in the name of 'competences', whether acquired, received or conferred.[42]

This does not mean that the criterion of competency (in terms of knowledge) defines a boundary between a dominant class and a dominated class. And it is not only a matter here of the existence of hybrid or intermediary positions. Later, (§3.1.1), we revisit the axiom according to which the class relationship defines not social groups but an *active* process of division: a division not in the sense of a distribution (*partition*), but in that of a *divisor*. Here, however, it is important to stress that from the moment one thinks in terms of an 'instrumentalisation of reason', one grasps that the

---

[42] Let's note – in contrast with some of Foucault's formulations, which seem to depart from facts of power insofar as they presuppose and produce facts of knowledge – a typical example: 'We cannot exercise power unless by the production of truth.' [Trans. – This sentence, situated on page 22 of the original French edition, is missing from the English translation but would otherwise be on p. 24 of *SD*.] The metastructural approach suggests an inverted theoretical order. Although knowledge and power condition each other reciprocally, we must – in the modern form of society – set out from knowledge and not from power in order to understand their relations of immanence. Since, knowledge (like property) forms the object of a *reproducible privilege* of power. Otherwise, which power is one speaking about? Power-domination exists only from the fact of these 'privileges'. The 'dominant' class is the class thus 'privileged'. It seems to me that by taking things in this way it is possible to identify the social forces in their presence.

people is not devoid of social *power*. And this is the case not merely because it forms a 'mass', but because it constitutes a rationally significant social force.[43] It does this in terms both of property and of competency. The fundamental class does not exist as such in modern society except insofar as it participates in socio-productive processes that are conjointly those of the market and organisation. In the wage relation, each person holds and asserts some right to make use of property on the *market*. And this is the case in accordance with a variable power of class, according to a configuration of hegemony between the three primary social forces, which determines the rules for wages, taxation, inheritance, etc. And each person also participates in expert *organisation,* which is the other element of the class relationship. The social functions of organisation and competency (teaching, technique, health, communication, etc.) do not *as such* belong to a dominant class – and nor does management [*encadrement*], which, moreover, is a point Marx himself had already stressed.[44] They are more or less instrumentalised, or more or less under a popular influence (power), which can be measured against the more or less

---

[43] See Mathieu Arnoux, *Le Temps des labourers: Travail, ordre social et crois-sance en Europe (11th–14th centuries),* Paris: Albin Michel, 2012. Arnoux highlights, counter to the stereotypical image of the passively exploited serf, the active part played by the peasantry in the European efflorescence.
[44] Marx, in chapter 13 of *Capital* on 'cooperation', underlines the 'in itself' rational character of organisation, together with the hierarchical elements that it contains, and which takes on a class character in the capi-talist factory. What he misses, in my view, is a measure of the fact that the 'class factor' thus constituted is not *defined by* capital: this is the *other fact,* which is to be found beyond its 'abolition'.

democratic nature of the rules that determine access to these functions and the modalities of their exercise. What Foucault notably shows is that not all power is to be found 'concentrated' at the summit: capitalist power is not independent of a state power that pertains to relations of force that traverse the entirety of the social fabric; and it follows from this that, for 'the people', *acceding to power* cannot simply mean 'taking power'. Neither ought we to forget that governing institutions also involve relations between the sexes, between the healthy and the ill, between generations, which are connected with, but irreducible to, class relations. In sum, we ought to dispense with the ill-posed question of knowing in which class to *classify* persons who occupy such-and-such a function, stratum or profession. That is not the object of class analysis, which instead aims at identifying social *processes*.

There nonetheless exists a range of social positions between those whose function is essentially one of management and *leadership* (power) and those who have as a vocation to accumulate and implement *competences* (knowledge). With no strict line of division between them, thus without being totally distinct from one another, some appear more as 'leaders', others more as 'experts'. The difference between them rather resides in that the former, notably in keeping with their position of *power* in capitalist production (and finance), find themselves closer to the pole of property, more or less sharing the exercise (and the earnings) of its specific power, whereas the latter, because *knowledge* is not as exclusive a 'property', are in a greater relation of continuity with the fundamental class.

To shine more light on the stakes of this 'micrological class relation', we ought to study the way in which 'class situation' opens onto differentiated 'class positions' (see §3.1.3). At this point of the analysis, let us simply remark, that Foucault aims his lens less at managers than at 'the competent'; not so much those who manage and direct material production, but those deemed competent in exercising a position in view of the 'good life' and of 'life' purely and simply: health, education, security, justice, mental hygiene, the management of bodies and souls. He situates them in their ambiguous position as purveyors of life and factors of subjectivation: at the juncture of 'reason-understanding' and of its 'instrumentalisation'.

But why speak of 'organisation' here? The 'pole' designated here as that of 'organisation' may seem inadequate to accommodating the Foucauldian figure of the doctor, the psychiatrist, the judge, etc. Foucault would have perhaps rejected the designation, with its evocations of structural rigidity.[45] To

---

[45] In Foucault's work, reference is nonetheless made to the idea of an *organisation* of society in its totality. See, for example, his lecture given in Tokyo in 1978 titled 'The analytic philosophy of politics'. In it he states that 'All the great disciplinary machineries, barracks, schools, workshops and prisons, are machines that make it possible to define the individual, to know who he is, what he does, what one can do with him, where one can place him and how to place him among others' (*DE3*/551). Significantly, Foucault ends up by grouping the 'struggles' linked to this as a specific whole, which he stresses merits as much attention as 'revolutionary struggles', by which is meant those that target 'economic power'. In short, he assuredly has in mind here a struggle for emancipation that is both a struggle against knowledge-power and a struggle against property-power. But the former of the two is the one that pertains to his object of study. And we will never be able to know exactly what he understood by the latter.

conceive the overall connection between more or less intentional social processes, more or less concerted practices of class or group – in contrast with the purely market mechanisms – he puts forward another body of concepts in terms '*apparatuses*' and '*strategies*'. He resists, as we will see (§§3.2.1–2), the idea of thinking on the basis of a structured totality. It nevertheless remains to be known whether one can understand the process of modern society in terms of Foucault's own version of fluid historicism; that is, if one can think of *strategy* without thinking in terms of *structure,* if one can think of structure without thinking of it in terms of *class* and think of *modern* class structure otherwise than on the basis of the instrumentalisation of the duality of market/organisation, where this latter claims a truth of means ordained toward the truth of its ends. These questions will return us to Marx, or rather to a meta-Marxist reconstruction of modern society.

In sum, this is the sense for me in the hypothesis that both Foucault's and Marx's works are to be read from this perspective of the 'instrumentalisation' of reason; that is, from that of its metastructural and bipolar 'market/organisation' content, which gives rise to the duality property-power and knowledge-power constitutive of the modern class relationship.[46] This is

---

[46] This 'meta-Marxist' approach is not without some analogy to the one that Étienne Balibar puts forward. 'Discipline, micro-power, represent then both the other aspect of capitalist exploitation and the other aspect of the juridico-political domination of class, the unity of which they enable us to conceive. This is to say, they come to be inserted exactly as the point of short-circuit performed by Marx between the economic and the political, society and the state, in his analysis of the production process' (*La*

naturally no more than an outline. Many points stand in need of further clarification.

2.3 FOUCAULT, HISTORIAN AND CRITIC OF 'COMPETENT-ELITES'

So, Foucault helps us to map the space of classes and of social forces. His history of 'truth' makes it possible to identify, alongside 'capital', 'another pole' of modern domination, one that, through knowledge-power, arrogates to itself the privilege of an agency of the 'true', which is also an agency of 'life'. One is nonetheless led to inquire into the conditions of the historical emergence of such a 'biopolitics', and more broadly into the historicity pertaining to it. In this sense I will investigate the sort of periodisation that Foucault brings to light in contrast to Marx, by seeking to go beyond both of them (§2.3.1). I will also examine the meaning taken in this context by the critique Foucault brings to bear on today's knowledge-power, in the name of what he referred to as a 'liberating' struggle (§2.3.2).

---

crainte des masses (Paris: Galilée, 1997), p. 297). For my part, however, I interpret discipline not as the other side of capitalism, but facing the latter, as pertaining to the other aspect (the other 'pole', which maintains a complex relation with the first) of class domination in modern society. Each of these two poles pertains at once to the economic and to the political: both 'poles' present two 'faces', and vice versa. What Balibar names, somewhat elliptically, a 'short-circuit', I analyse in terms of the 'metastructural grid' presented above in the Introduction, an analytical grid for the study of class relationships in modern society.

2.3.1 The historical conditions of modern 'biopolitics'

For all times, political power is presumed to protect the life of those who recognise it – that is, at least, its legitimation. But, if this is what it does, it is classically by means of a certain monopoly of violence, which itself relies upon a certain order of custom or right. By 'biopolitics', Foucault means the public 'taking in charge' of life – of health, food, hygiene, birth, sexuality, etc. – and he seeks to identify its historical stages. He employs this term regarding the pre-liberal institutions of the 'police', in the old sense of the term, that organisational practice of government in the service of the power of states. But he applies it in privileged fashion to the 'liberalism' of the second half of the eighteenth century, which impels this biopolitics in a direction that will only continue to amplify until the present day. He thus opens a fruitful historical path. It seems to me, however, that one benefits by taking a step back, by searching further back in modern experience. Were the Chinese emperors not also, notably since the so-called 'modern' era, that is, since the Song, preoccupied with public prosperity (irrigation, canals …), health, agricultural techniques, education and urbanism? I return below (§4.2.2) to the liberal moment and to the form of biopolitical productivity that Foucault attributes to it. But I would first like to suggest that we can, by returning to the initial experiences of European modernity, set Foucault's investigation within a broader temporality proper to the interpretation of present times, those of neoliberal 'altimodernity'.[47]

---

[47] See the conclusion of *Le Néolibéralisme, Un autre grand récit*, Paris: Les Prairies Ordinaires, 2016, entitled 'Le néolibéralisme, seuil d'une ultimodernité'.

Let us, then, reflect upon the first modern 'socio-political' attempt, namely that of the north Italian commune of the thirteenth century, in which what received specific crystallisation, owing to a conjuncture in which the weakening of royal and imperial tutelage made it possible to go 'to the end', was an experience that would remain un-accomplished elsewhere in European medieval space.[48] We discover in it, closely correlated with a juridical-political foundation established by modern republican institutions, a positively 'biopolitical' orientation, in the sense of the public management of use-values comprising collective life. *On the one hand,* in effect, what is sketched for the first time in Europe in the form of the city-state is a *claim* to live together under a 'regime of speech' according to which 'one voice equals one voice' (within the limits of the exclusion of women, the poorest and foreigners, which are abiding givens ...). In it, popular sovereignty is regularly refounded through the elaboration of a constitution in the framework of an elected legislative assembly, presumed to control the executive ('podestat', a foreigner dedicated to public interest alone) – such is at least the declared claim and the object of struggles of power. But there is 'another face', an economic one, of this modern emergence; and this is decisive as regards the hypothesis elaborated by Foucault. The people of the city, by being organised into corporations (in *arti*), managed – at least in the most favourable circumstances – to achieve some kind of

---

[48] This is the topic of chapter 7 of my *L'État-monde,* pp. 188–232.

collective control over economic processes. Its sovereign claim was not limited to the *political* domain but also concerned – a fact that is unprecedented and a notable point of difference with respect to the democracies of Antiquity – economic *life* itself in all its aspects.

The new apparatus of 'life' included not only supply, an old problem for cities, but – a novel thing – the organisation of commerce, the supervision of the corporations, price controls, taxation (made proportionate to wealth, invention of the *estimo*), infrastructure and urbanism, the school system, the armed forces and diplomacy, population control (control notably of urban immigration) and finally the law itself through the very first emergence of an inquisitorial legal system (according to which crimes and offences *damage* [le sent] *the social body*), as well as also religion in its civic form. This is well and truly a 'police', *Polizei*, in the classic sense of the term, which finds itself thus constituted in the new concepts of the 'common', the 'common good', 'common utility', which converge towards majestic 'palaces of reason'. Everything is set for an increase in the power of the city-state in the competitive system of a nascent modern world system. That this proto-democratic experience is still only a matter of an oligarchic power (encircled by the feudal order and interlocking with it) does not prevent the emergence – more or less marked but *in a single go,* and in a Christianity where the old social relations are still fated to prevail for some time – of a *set* of modern features, ones that prefigure those that Foucault evokes concerning the seventeenth century and the

first half of the eighteenth century.[49] When a specific power of
the city can act to curb vendettas between nobles through law,
their monopoly on legitimate violence or the omnipotence
of the 'magnates', who were excluded from the city for being
'rapacious wolves', the juridico-political already opens on
to biopolitical terrain: the negativity of the law is translated
into the positivity of life. This revolutionary experience was
of course ephemeral. But it is indicative of a new field of
possibilities that presented its specific coherence, that of a
buon governo, which would progressively come to be asserted
over ever larger spaces – and which carried over, moreover,
many of the oligarchic features inherent to the modern
structuration of class (with the 'republican' institution suited
to it), of which it constitutes the first sketch.[50] The proto-
modernity of the Italian commune – at least this is what I've
tried to show – resides in this public and private interference
in *market* and *organisation,* in which the public discourse that
interposes between them and emerges from this confrontation
– as the immediacy between these two mediations – takes as

---

[49] In *Psychiatric Power,* Foucault significantly underlines the fact that
'disciplinary power' appears in the religious communities of the Second
Middle Ages of the Communes – of the first emergence of the 'modern
form of society' – and generalised from the seventeenth to eighteenth
centuries. See notably pp. 63–91. Significantly also, the first measure
taken by the Ciompi in revolt was directed against the system of torture
that Foucault made the mark of the *Ancien Régime.* See Alessandro Stella,
La Révolte des Ciompi, Paris: Editions de l'EHESS, 1993.
[50] On the continuity of the communal imaginary, even when it turned, as
it did in Florence or Milan, against the *popolo,* see Patrick Boucheron, *Le
Monde en 1500,* Paris: Fayard, 2009, pp. 62–3.

its object *the material life* of those who uphold it. This is the sense in which what appears, in this moment and in this place, is a 'socio-political' modernity in which 'society' seeks to take control of 'politics' in the sense that 'the people', or at least its outline in the '*popolo*', gives itself the aim of mastering the vital processes of this interference between these two mediations.

This foray into historiography suggests that the confrontation between Marx and Foucault concerning an interpretation of modern times should be begun anew from a point further back in history.

In Marx's view, as we know, the framework of this interpretation is set by the relations between the 'productive forces' and the 'relations of production': to each determined technological level there corresponds a particular mode (slave state, feudal, capitalist...) wherein a specific fraction of the social body is able to appropriate for itself the essential means of production and make the masses work to its advantage. But, correlatively, this structural aptitude to govern production manifests an ability to foster the subsequent development of the productive forces, to the point that they cause that particular structure of social domination to break apart. Then we arrive at the times of new social revolutions.

Foucault resists this type of 'historical dialectic', rightfully suspecting that it harbours an ad hoc construction that is geared to staging the plausibility of a 'passage to socialism'. It is true that completely other things can be found in Marx, such as the sequence leading from manufacture to large-scale industry, which makes possible an interrogation into what occurs when one passes to a later technological stage. Whatever the case, we are left with the contrast between Marx, who conceives the historical *tendency* from the dynamic immanent to the social *structure,* and Foucault, who inflects historicity in terms of singular, heterogeneous novelties, such as the successive phases of the history of political reason: state of justice, administrative state, era of government. The periodisations that he puts forward bring to light an entirely different face of history, one left in the shadows by Marxism. It may be, however, that the historical framework on which he embroiders, presents the opposite bias to that of Marx, who accounts for modern history on the basis of the movement of *capital.* Foucault thinks on the basis of the pole of power-knowledge: the anatomo-political in the seventeenth century, the biopolitical in the eighteenth, oriented discipline, then oriented control, changes of episteme, of orders of reason. One is brought to wonder how these approaches could be accounted for within a broader concept.

The historiography of the Italian commune justifies, in my view, the project to renew thinking on the basis of the hypothesis I have called 'metastructural'. By accounting for the 'modern form of society' founded upon the 'instrumentalisation of reason' – understood according to its two poles, 'between-individuals' in the market and 'between-everyone' in organisation – as given in its logical coherence from its medieval beginning, thus in a world that would still long be dominated by other social logics, one puts oneself, it seems to me, in a position to approach an understanding of the *historical incoherence* of modern times. For, why does one see emerge, over the centuries of the (still unfinished) construction of modernity, here a state bureaucracy (the Italy of the Renaissance, the Germany of the *Länder*), there a land-owning and then industrial bourgeois class (England), there again a state nobility (France), and all this without preventing the other constitutive features of this structure from manifesting in each scenario, albeit in minor mode, before they eventually come to form the 'overarching tableau' evoked by Foucault and that we rediscover today, despite multiple inequalities and discrepancies, from one nation state to another? The metastructural hypothesis is that this sequence of eras is to be understood in terms of 'changes of hegemony': in the sense that what by turns comes to dominate, against the backdrop of technological mutations, is one or other of the two social forces (one centred on the market, the other on organisation) constitutive of the dominant class, in accordance with fluctuations in their *structural* connections to the fundamental class and with *systemic* (i.e. global) contexts in incessant upheaval.[51]

The Foucauldian conception – in contrast with Marx's, which centres on the property-power of capital – provides us with a better understanding of the specific part played by knowledge-power in all these processes. Ever since its medieval beginnings, the modern state has of course proclaimed its concern with the life of people, notably by *protecting* the

---

51 This theory of hegemony will be put forward in *Le Néolibéralisme, Un autre grand récit*, Paris: Les Prairies Ordinaires, 2016.

population from the violence threatening it (by exercising its own …), thus ensuring the operation of institutions that gave economic and cultural coherence to the then emerging territorialities. In some places one can see an early emergence of the postulates of a 'police' still to come. But, starting in the classical era, conjoint to the *market* development of capitalism, one can also observe a parallel rise in the *organisational* capacity of the social body, as the fruit and factor of burgeoning knowledges and techniques; that is, an aptitude to design and implement collective ends in the various domains of existence. Knowledge-power thereby comes to be exercised and reproduced through a set of always more complex and interrelated social functions, which impact the intellectual and corporeal life of all, in accordance with successive thresholds. Foucault shows how this knowledge-power operates at the juncture of relations of production, health, justice, gender and family, by becoming involved in the use of use-values, in the use of the producing, suffering, enjoying body – in a word, in the use of self. He decodes this biopolitical charge, which increases over the course of modern times, and the claims to which it gives rise.[52]

---

[52] In a society in which power asserts its orientation toward the common good, there comes a moment when the mad person and the delinquent appear, certainly, as dangerous individuals, but as individuals that one has a duty to cure or improve. The alienist doctors thus came to appropriate the 'crimes' of mad people in the name of 'public hygiene', maintaining that madness is a danger that the doctor only can diagnose. See *PK*/204–5. In times of science, this is how knowledge-power is advanced.

2.3.2 The Foucauldian critique
of knowledge-power: a politics

Foucault thus truly formulates a *class* critique. If traditional Marxism struggles to recognise it, this is because it takes aim not at 'capital', but at the other pole of the dominant class: at the institutions and practices by which that *other* power is exercised, and, within this latter, at the aspect of 'competency'. Foucault develops a politics on this basis. And whatever may be his desire for rupture, he reiterates a certain view of the social whole without which politics is inconceivable.[53]

In an interview with K. S. Karol (*FL*190ff.), Foucault notes that the Soviets adopted techniques that the 'bourgeoisie' had invented. By this he meant not techniques of the market but those of the other 'pole' of modern 'bourgeois' power, that is, of organisation. 'Traditional Marxism', he said, considers prison and the asylum as *marginal* facts. One does not completely go against Foucault's thinking by defining them, on the contrary, as *structural* processes. The problem, in his view, is not so much to know if Marxism has any scientific value than it is to 'question ourselves about our aspirations as to the kind of power that is presumed to accompany such a science' (*PK/84*).

---

[53] Jose Luis Moreno Pestāna, *Foucault, la gauche et la politique*, Paris: Editions Textuel, 2010, suggests a detailed analysis of Foucault's itinerary. And Gérard Noiriel has done a study on the modalities of Foucault's intellectual engagement ('Les trois figures de l'intellectuel engagé', in Marie-Christine Grandjonc, ed., *Penser avec Michel Foucault*, Paris: Karthala, 2005). My ambition is different: namely I seek to establish a mode of communication between the respective politics inspired by Marx and by Foucault.

His interest bears on Soviet 'Marxism' as knowledge that is born out as power. By establishing itself as a science, Marxism becomes drawn into the programme of research into the effects of power that, since the Middle Ages, the West 'has reserved for those who uphold a scientific discourse' (*PK/85*; tm). In the USSR, the entire state network worked to enforce a form of Marxist knowledge-power and, in so doing, managed to carry a potentiality of 'western' society to term. Apart from the 'effects of power' that attach to property, Foucault thus sheds light on those that attach to the other process *of class* inherent in modern society, that of knowledge-power.

> This form of power is exercised on immediate everyday life, categorising individuals, designating them by their own individuality, attaching them to their own identities, imposing on them a law of truth that they must recognise and others have to recognise in them. It is a form of power that transforms individuals into subjects. There are two meanings of the word 'subject': subject to someone else by control and dependence, and tied to one's own identity by a conscience or self-knowledge. Both meanings suggest a form of power that subjugates and makes subject to. (*EWF3/331*)

At issue is not so much 'to attack such-and-such an institution of power, or group or class or elite but instead a particular technique, a form of power', made up of 'multiple, indefinite relations of power' (ibid.). Corresponding to this, as one ought to add in keeping with good nominalist logic, is a set of agents that in actual fact contains the entire array of professions, the discourses and practices of which Foucault analyses.

I leave aside here the question of knowing if the 'transformation of individuals into subjects' is specifically the business of this 'sort of power' or if it is not rather necessary to relate it to a more complex and dialectical game of markets and organisational class and state relations. At this point we can already claim, however, that Foucault here opens a new chapter of class struggle.[54] This chapter is one of resistance to the strategies specific to knowledge-power: 'transversal', 'immediate', 'anarchic' struggles. These forms of resistance do not seek out the 'chief enemy', but rather the 'immediate enemy' – that is, not the power of capital but that of competent knowledge. 'They pit their resistance against the effects of power linked with knowledge, competence and qualification. They fight against the privileges of knowledge' (*EWF3*/330; tm). Foucault offers them, following a metaphor that Deleuze also uses (*FL*/76), his 'box of tools' to assist them in 'breaking up the systems of power' (*FL*/149).

This does not signify the stigmatisation of knowledge-power per se, which is devoid of a pre-established political function. The power that proceeds from knowledge bears a specific capacity (*puissance*). To restate this in metastructural terms: it pertains to a mode of rational-reasonable coordination at the social scale, and which is such only by its coordination

---

54 See notably his article 'The Subject and Power' (1982), *EWF3*/330–1.

of rational-reasonable beings. It is would thus be extinguished as a 'power' properly speaking, as political relation, were it to become a pure instrumentalisation. The prerogatives of management in the enterprise or the administration, the requirement of obedience, manipulation and intimidation itself – all this is exercised against the backdrop of class violence, in a form of society that otherwise (but there is nothing incidental about it), and contradictorily, declares the liberty-equality-rationality of all. And in this regard knowledge-power adopts a position different to that of property-power. *It manifests itself only by communicating itself,* with retroactive effect. This occurs under conditions that, it is true, are vastly unequal, whether inside administrations, schools, enterprises or the army, to say nothing of the prison or the psychiatric hospital. It is formative of the knowing subject, and transformative of the subject that its knowledge bears upon and that it addresses, a subject that reacts to it in turn. So, little wonder that in Foucault we find – as the counterpart to a history of truth that deciphers the effects of violence linked to competency – an *interpellation* of today's experts. He addresses them as 'specific intellectuals', endowed with a specific knowledge-power, insofar as they work not 'within the universal' but 'in determinate sectors', in their sites and on their objects of work. Doing this, he claims, they ultimately encounter 'the same adversary as the proletariat, the peasantry or the masses (the multinationals, the juridical and police apparatus, real estate speculation) …'. In short, they are apt to be mobilised against the 'chief enemy'. They are no longer writers, but instead 'magistrates and psychiatrists, doctors and social workers, laboratory technicians and sociologists' etc. (*PK*/127). These holders of knowledge-power find themselves, in contrast with the privileged agents of property-power, in a class situation open to contrary 'class positions': the 'petit-bourgeois in the service of capitalism' or else the 'organic intellectual of the proletariat' (*PK*/132). They choose their camp. And this is true of Foucault himself, who does not fail to underline the link between his work of theoretical elaboration and the singular experience that he had on the heels of '68.

It is true that one's understanding of the event in which he is situated around the 1970s may differ from that suggested by his writings at the time.[55] After the end of an 'alliance', of a 'collusion' between competent-elites and the popular classes that harked back to the major upheavals of the 1930s, a sort of acme was reached in diverse places around the globe. New fractions of experts, whose number multiplied, engaged in battle against capitalist power, 'the chief enemy', as part of an unprecedented class struggle, and nevertheless in parallel to that of the 'workers' movement'. Just as the revolutionaries of 1793 discovered accents of the ancient republics, the 'leftists'– students who were future experts and sure of it –

---

55 When, for example, in an interview in *Partisan Review* in Spring 1971, he said about the struggle of American students that, 'the advantage in America is that there are no large conservative forces like the Communist Party and the CGT. By prohibiting and prosecuting the Communist Party for so many years, I think that the American government has, in a sense, done a favour to the revolutionary cause: it kept open the possibility of ties between students and workers' ('A Conversation with Michel Foucault', conducted by John K. Simon, April–June 1971, in *Power/Knowledge*, pp. 37–54)

adopted the repertoire of proletarian revolution. Foucault initially displays his astonishment that the students 'only talk about class struggle'. But he wastes no time in adopting this language himself.[56] His scholarly investigations, which lead him to forge the concept of discipline, find their inspiration in it. The emancipatory struggle of specific intellectuals in fact turned naturally against its opposite: against the hierarchical power of competency, which puts the exercise of competency at the service of bourgeois power. The neoliberal tumult would not take long to arrive, and many a sharp mind would change position. But this struggle, which in diverse places caused an upheaval within institutions as well as within culture, continues to be a powerful heritage.

In this obscure melee, Foucault promptly took a stand against the Communist Party, which was centred on the

---

[56] The interview that he gives in *L'Arc* (no. 49, 1972) – 'Intellectuals and Power' – in the company of Deleuze, the watchword of which is the refusal to 'totalise' the relations between 'theory and practice', gives leftism its letters of nobility. Theory and practice can only ever be local. 'Each struggle develops around a particular source of power (any of the countless, tiny sources—a small-time boss, the manager of an HLM [Low Income Housing], a prison warden, a judge, a union representative, the editor-in-chief of a newspaper). [...] designating the target is the first step for other struggles against power' (*FL*/79). The militant frenzy that suddenly seizes hold of these two great minds against all sorts of 'minor figures' is no less than that shown by Althusser in his declarations of fidelity to his party, which are to be found, it is true, in a text that remained unpublished. They strive to outdo one another with their references to the 'proletariat' and the 'revolutionary movement of the proletariat' (p. 81). This somewhat incantational pathos takes nothing away from the theoretical and practical part that they took in the struggles of prisoners and other then-emergent 'uprisings'. Nonetheless, it overcodes the set of remarks.

working class and beholden to an arena in which the fight waged is one against capital, from which one struggles to understand the process in its entirety. What occurs at the 'other pole' remains, in its purview, marginal. Foucault, for his part, had a completely different perception of the 'great battle', in which he participated from the viewpoint of another site, which is to say, precisely, knowledge-power. This 'great battle' does not arise from the progression of a grand History, which, opposing labour (and with it the people) to capital, is placed under the aegis of a working class endowed with a universal vocation, and therefore in a natural (or mystical) relation with intellectuals, whose function it is to speak the universal. Instead it is made up – in the multiplicity of its wellsprings – of events, of previously unseen things, of many beginnings in various social fields that are out of sync with one another. It is this sense in which the Foucauldian 'genealogy' is proffered as a history written from the viewpoint of the combat of the oppressed (*PK*/65). However, the understanding here is that this 'battle' can gain consistency only when nourished by subversive knowledge formed through interference between specific, intellectual forms of knowledge and the local knowledge peculiar to the actors concerned and that arises from their particular struggles.

It will be noted that in these 'specific struggles' 'specific intellectuals' take a leading role. For, in Foucault's view, this 'specificity' does not mean that the search for good strategy is to take place among the diverse spontaneity of 'exemplary struggles'. As the theoretician of a 'history of truth', he also emerges as the herald of a 'politics of truth',

which is the 'function' of intellectuals, and more specifically
of philosophy.[57] This amounts to another way of taking up
Marx's expression according to which 'philosophy must
come back down to the earth', and the philosopher – the
'great intellectual'? – must establish himself at the centre of
politics. The specific intellectual sets his sights well beyond
his professional universe: 'he fights at the general level of this
regime of truth, so essential to the structures and functioning
of our society'. In this way the specific communicates with
the universal; and the power of knowledge with the power
of emancipation. This comes pretty close to reclaiming the
primary role for intellectuals (despite appeals for 'proletarian'
leadership). Says Foucault, 'It's not a matter of liberating truth
from every system of power – that would be a chimera since
truth is already power – but of detaching the power of truth
from the (social, economic, cultural) forms of hegemony
within which it operates at the present time' (PK/132–3). As
we see, the boundary between the universal intellectual and the
specific intellectual recedes here somewhat. Foucault's pathetic
address to the canonical intellectual – pleading for 'him to take

---

[57] On this basis, the proximity between Foucault and the Frankfurt
School, which Foucault understands as a philosophical project, is significant. See Emmanuel Renault, 'Foucault et l'École de Francfort', in Yves
Cusset et Stéphane Haber (eds.) *Habermas et Foucault,* Paris: CNRS,
2006, pp. 55–68. Renault shows that Foucault, who encounters this
tradition around 1978, at the moment of its reception in France, quickly
adopts its critical themes. 'But', he remarks, 'a more precise interpretation suggests that Foucault has more immediately in mind Horkheimer's
Traditional and Critical Theory, or even that while discussing the School's
themes he attributes them to Kant' (p. 65).

leave of the prophetic function of the intellectual derived from the notable' (*EWF3*/128) – marks a posture of which he himself was a brilliant exponent. His wily political rhetoric, his incisive formulas, in which the touch of obscurity and vagueness that signal prophecy remains, were part of a scene on which the respective merits of Sartre and … of some worthy successor were being played out.

Within the space of a few decades, the once-bold distinctions between diverse and (at the time) rival projects of emancipatory struggle – emerging from movements that appeared in various times and places of the modern social configuration – have come to seem less clear cut. The 'intellectuals' who joined communist parties learned, if were it still unclear to them, that they were expected to front up for 'specific' struggles around teaching, research, the press, the hospital, justice, etc. They were firmly urged to keep to this 'specific' role, to desist from their natural propensity to act as an elite headquarters. They were denied all privileges … The 'workers' movement', as an organised apparatus, privileged two types of discipline: *the economy,* directed at drawing up political platforms based on the collective appropriation of the means of production, and *history* and *philosophy* – a philosophy of history – geared towards promoting a humanist and revolutionary vision of the world. No 'sociology' made its way into this 'specific' programme. 'Leftism' thus arose from social space that escaped this movement's outlook. It was symptomatic of the opening of new fronts operating outside the orbit of the 'working class'. It was sociologically apt to inspire multidisciplinary experiences, to which the properly unclassifiable work of Foucault came to be a reference.

The militant groups and parties from those times have all but vanished from public space. History's course seems to have been reversed. The cards of social criticism have fallen in thousands of ways. The new debates introduced by neoliberal globalisation mix in with those that such criticism carries in procession, on liberty, equality, justice ... Yet the old cultural and political antagonisms continue to operate, since they stem from *structural* divisions that are constitutive of modern society; they are the wellsprings of a variety of historical experiences to which Marx and Foucault remain, in their various ways, privileged witnesses. The contours of a possible encounter nonetheless begin to take shape: the theoretical breakthrough marked by the concept of power-knowledge enables us to glimpse not only the possibility of broadening the Marxian theory of classes for modern society, but also its refoundation on a more realistic and assured basis. If this is right, we might thereby be able to clarify the nature of the difficulties that strategies of emancipation encounter. As we shall see, this is the end towards which the considerations I engage in here tend. Nonetheless, a certain number of epistemological obstacles still stand in the way, which we must now attempt to tackle.

3

MARXIAN STRUCTURALISM AND FOUCAULDIAN NOMINALISM?

When undertaking to establish an apposite relationship between the respective worlds of Marx and Foucault, the first obstacle we come up against is philosophical in nature, namely the supposed chasm between 'nominalism', or the primacy given to the singular, which governs the Foucauldian analysis of *power,* and 'structuralism', or holist realism, which is held to characterise the notions of *class* and *state* as conceived in the Marxist tradition. The 'structuralism' attributed to Marx here refers not to the idea that society is 'structured like a language', but to the notion of 'class *structure'* contained in the distinction he makes between base and superstructure. Structure is that which, reproducing itself, constitutes a stable form of society, and which nonetheless contains immanent tendencies that open onto a determinate field of possibles. So Marxism examines, at least according to one view of it, the givenness of particular individuals in a society on the basis of the social structures in which they are inserted. This is the way in which Marxian structuralism appears opposed to Foucault's assertion of nominalism (§3.1). Of note is the manifest gap between the Foucauldian analysis in terms of 'apparatuses of power' and the ambition, sparked by Marx's theory, to analyse the social on the basis of the social whole, understood in terms of 'class structure' (§3.2). How are we to conceive the relation between society and individuals? This classic problem of sociology, dramatised with reference to two heterogeneous philosophies, here takes an acute form. However, is it legitimate, with regard to the conceptual work to which these two oeuvres attest, to confine Marx to a realism of structures and Foucault to a nominalism of beings and things? Is it possible to set against one another the two political paths that seem to emerge from such an alternative? And in which terms can we attempt the theoretical test that might lead us, beyond all eclecticism, to adopt them both as elements, discordant but inseparable ones, of a political path in which the great diversity of forms of social subversion can be recognised? A critical analysis of the limits inherent to each of these conceptual frameworks, which shows the impossibility of integrating them within a general theory, presents itself as an essential prerequisite (§3.3).

3.1 MICRO-RELATIONS OF POWER AND MACRO-RELATIONSHIPS OF CLASS

Let us first consider the conceptual sites – of power in Foucault and of class in Marx – over which structuralism and nominalism clash most explicitly. Both perspectives presuppose one another. Such will be the hypothesis at least (§3.1.1). Yet it happens that its pertinence can be shown only if into the Marxian structuralist concept of social 'relationship' [*rapport*] one can integrate a Foucauldian nominalist concept of singular 'relation' [*relation*]: that is to say, to conceive, correlative to the *class relationship* (which is macrological), *class relations* (which are micrological, inter-individual) (§3.1.2); which is also to be understood as a (micrological) *relation to the state* (§3.1.3). This points us toward a form of dialectic that is yet to be defined.

Let's note that the French language happens to have two different terms to express this distinction (*rapport, relation*), where English only has one (relation). To be sure, the meanings of these French terms are somewhat irresolute: one could just as easily turn things around and speak of '*relationships*' between *individuals* and of '*relations*' between *classes*. But the linguistic tradition of the human sciences pleads for a contrary view; for it, 'relation' suggests a nominalist context and '*relationship*' a structuralist one. This little linguistic fact facilitates our formulation of the problem.

3.1.1 The Foucauldian concept of power and the Marxian concept of class

Foucault sought on many occasions to expound on his conception of power, most notably in an article from 1982, 'The Subject and Power' (*EWF3*/326–48). Power, he writes there, must be considered as the action of an individual on the action of other individuals. Hence the 'transitive' meaning that he gives to the concept of 'government': to govern the conduct of others. These actions, he adds, are to be grasped as operating within a field of socially given possibilities in networks of institutions and all order of relations, and in all the domains of social life: family, production, health, education, police and justice, war, etc. The state is only the general 'envelop' within which these multiple relations, insofar as they are relations of power, come to be regulated in one way or another. What Foucault refuses is the idea that we must begin with the state institution understood as the site of a power that would be exercised either by transferring the individual's rights to the collective or by consent obtained through violence. He understands the state, qua site of violence and consent, on the basis of the micro-relations of power immanent to every social relation. 'When I evoke the operations of power', he writes, 'I refer not only to the problem of the state apparatus, of the ruling class, of hegemonic castes [...] but to an entire series of increasingly fine, microscopic powers, which are exercised on individuals in their daily conduct and right down to the level of their own bodies' (*DE2*/771).[1] This stands in contrast, he continues, to Althusser and his notion of 'ideological state apparatuses'.[2]

---

[1] This is also the sense of the recurrent metaphor of 'capillary power' developed, notably in *Psychiatric Power* (p. 40), to characterise the disciplinary power 'specific to our society'. It aims at 'the terminal form of power', as it were, at the moment it comes to 'reach the level of bodies and seize hold of them'.

[2] In this regard, the reader will note that the tone of the reference to Althusser corresponds to Foucault's increasing distance from Marxism.

It is in this sense that, in an interview conducted in July 1977, Foucault acquiesces to Jacques Alain Miller's suggestion that, 'ultimately, the first and last element is that of individuals', who are grouped into 'provisional coalitions', which are more or less lasting (*PK*/208; tm). This micro-logical approach enables us, he says, to understand chance 'much better than in other theoretical procedures for grasping the relation that exists between power and struggles, and especially class struggle'. What is in effect striking in the Marxist texts, he adds with a slight provocation, is that in speaking of class struggle 'one passes over in silence precisely what is meant by struggle'. It is at this micro level that one can grasp the idea that 'civil society is riven by class struggle' (*ibid.*). As he puts it, 'There aren't

---

I return below to his 1971 interview, conducted in dialogue with Noam Chomsky, in which this distance is not marked.

In his lectures at the Collège de France in 1973, *The Punitive Society,* he puts to Althusser, in still rather muted terms, that there exists 'an entire set of [other] sources of powers, which can be sexual relations, the family, employment, housing' (*SPu*/234). In 1975, he claims to be ready 'to consider these problems, then to reintegrate them into the old question of the state apparatus' (*DE2*/772). In 1977, he again asserts the opposition of both approaches.

In fact, however, Althusser was also very attentive to the dissemination of power within the pores of society: everything is political, and there-fore also a state relation of power. Far from endorsing an understand-ing of state power from the viewpoint of its summit, he puts forward a 'provisional' list of 'ideological state apparatuses' – educational, familial, religious, political, union apparatuses, as well as those related to infor-mation, publishing, culture – which potentially spread throughout all the blood vessels of social life (see *On Reproduction,* Paris: PUF, 2005, p. 234). As such, the chasm between both approaches is of another nature: whereas Althusser is only interested in the *ideological hold* that these 'apparatuses' ensure, Foucault discerns in them *the production of knowl-edges,* of knowledge-power.

immediately given subjects of the struggle, one the proletariat, the other the bourgeoisie. Who fights against whom? We all fight against each other. And there is always something in each of us that fights against something else in each of us' (ibid.; tm).

We might note, however, that this does not prevent Foucault from regularly invoking the 'structures' that, in the background, form the 'frameworks' or 'supports' of individual interactions. Power is not 'something' that exists as 'global, massive or diffused; concentrated or distributed', he writes, 'even though, of course, [...] permanent structures do underpin it' (EWF3/340). This treatment in terms of 'even though' or 'not only', a recurrent feature of Foucault's discourse, boils down to situating the 'structures', thus evoked in a purely trivial fashion, outside his field of analysis. However, we ought not omit to inquire into the possible relations between these two terms, individual and structure. And as for Foucault the notion of structure refers to a Marxist perspective, from which he seeks to take a distance, one is led to ask how this issue plays out in Marx. Marx's account contains a certain difficulty in this regard, which comes to light, for example, in chapter 12 of Capital, when he puts forward a distinction between the 'essence', or 'inner law', that would be entailed in the class relation, understood as the *relationship* between two classes (capitalists and wage earners), and the 'phenomenon', which we must here understand to mean the *relation* of competition between individual capitalists within their own class. Accordingly, Marx stresses that where common sense is absorbed in the phenomenon (Erscheinung, το φαινόμενον, 'that which appears'), capitalism is given as a society of competition, a *market* society. He intends here to put the accent on that which is 'essential', i.e. which appears only within a theoretical construction: this is the relationship between classes, the relationship of class (exploitation), which, expressed as the accumulation of surplus value, constitutes the foundation of capitalism. The objection may be raised that the *market* relation is absolutely *essential* to this *capitalist relationship,* and competition is *essential* to the historical dynamic of capital – indeed, it pertains to its very 'essence'. Moreover, this also comes through in the set-up of Marx's own account, which begins with the market, or inter-individual aspect (Book 1, Section 1), before moving on to the capitalist class *relationship* (Section 3), which 'transforms' this presupposed market *relation* between individuals, but does not substitute it. Therein lies the entire problem. And the duality 'essence/phenomenon', in the uncertain usage Marx makes of it here, reveals a difficulty in conceiving the connection between the inter-individual relation and the class relationships.[3]

It would be incorrect to think that Marx can be confined to a holistic schema. The notion of 'class in itself', *qua* that which

---

[3] This is why I once described it as an 'epistemological support-obstacle'. See *Que faire du Capital?*, pp. 133–42 and 168ff. In this passage, Marx purports to postpone the study of competition, whereas it is on the basis of it (and rightly so), on the basis of an analysis of *differential* surplus value – result of the *relation* of competition between capitalists – that he explains the productive dynamic leading to *relative* surplus value, which, through the concentration of capital, sets in motion the *relationship* between both classes. This terminological wavering, which reveals an aim that priori-tises the 'relationship' over the 'relation', has the value of a symptom.

would need only to become aware of itself in order to become a 'class for itself', is an operator of political action: it stresses that the conditions do exist under which to gather together. It does not mean that *classes* can be circumscribed into social *groups*. The class relationship, such as it is inscribed in *Capital*, designates not a group but a *split,* a principle of division of the social body. The mechanism of exploitation establishes, at the heart of society, a *cut* that governs the social dynamic in the last instance. But it does not translate into two social *groups*: it *gives rise* to groups, to *groupings,* which are – in accordance with the variability of relations of force that it determines in variable conjunctures – essentially fluid (this is the sense, moreover, in which one could reinterpret the class 'in itself' and 'for itself', if one thinks at least that this philosophical recourse adds something to an understanding of the process). The 'great industrial patronat' or the 'industrial working class', *qua* the two social *groups* in which class division had a dominant place in Europe in the twentieth century, have seen the time of their importance wane in the face of 'finance' and other 'proletariats'. But the capitalist class relationship – what we generally call 'the social classes' – remains the pivotal point of the becoming of society: it *gives rise* to other groupings, to other groups in struggle. 'Class struggle' is thus to be used as a sort of abbreviation. In class struggle, it is not the classes that struggle, but individuals who belong to social groups that determine this class division as a function of the circumstances (technological and other). These groups aggregate persons who are gathered together on account of a set of shared social conditions, which also affect each person differently. Class division passes through individuals themselves (something Foucault also emphasised in his own way: 'there is always something in us that struggles against something else in us'). To each person a particular horizon, an always more or less uncertain one, is opened in a complex and overdetermined set of singular, fluctuating biographical conditions (familial, geographical and professional). On the other hand, just as Foucault stresses about the holders of knowledge-power, a social (class) *situation* does not necessarily define a political (class) *position*. Nor are these simply facts attributable to the inexhaustible contingency of empirical reality: theory has to strive to account for certain regular occurrences.[4] But, in short, *class is created in such a way that it is always necessary to look in it for the individual in his or her exceptionality.* Class comprises only exceptional individuals in singular situations.

What remains to be shown is the cost of thinking this through: under which conditions is the inter-individual *relation* included in the overall *relationship,* and vice versa?

3.1.2 The micro-macrological articulation of class

In ordinary everyday consciousness, the individual appears as a primary given. Foucault and Marx duly note this, each in his own way. Foucault repeats that 'of course' structures exist

---

[4] This is one of the topics of chapter 4 of *L'État-monde,* 'Class, parti et mouvements'. In it, I attempt to provide an answer to the question of the gap between the social composition of parties and the classes that they claim to represent.

in the background, but does so without working them into his research programme. So, despite carrying out a powerful critique of structuralism, he tends to remain confined to a nominalism of common sense that does not submit to the test of the collective – or, at least, does not revisit the point at which inter-individual arrangements specifically require thinking through in modern society, which is to say, as part of modern class division. Marx, for his part, underlines the idea that immediate experience (the 'phenomenon', that which 'appears' from the outset) does not supply the key to social theory. But he does mean for his theory of the class *relationship* to treat concrete individuals, *relations* between singular subjects. In my view, however, he achieves this imperfectly. This is because the juncture between structuralism and nominalism requires a *transformation* of the Marxian matrix of class: that put forward in the metastructural approach that Marx initiated but failed to follow through on.

At §3.1.1 above, I embarked on this path by indicating that class is not a group: the class relation is first to be understood as a *division* within the modern social body, *one that gives rise to social groups,* groups that gather together singular persons to varying degrees. But this is only the negative, external moment of the analysis.

Prior to tackling the positive moment that emerges from the metastructural approach, it pays once more to revisit the difficulties involved in the recognition of the fact of 'classes'. I would like to show that *it is because classes are invisible* (at least in terms of what they are) *that the relation between the individual moment and the moment of class is so difficult to perceive.* In the duality individual/class, it is the second term that is most elusive, and this makes their relation elusive.

The main difficulty resides in the fact that, in contrast with *social groups,* which are entities of the same kind, and although they distinguish themselves via specific features (interests, lifestyles, ideologies, etc.), *classes* lack that 'family resemblance' that would make it possible to 'visualise' them as part of the same concept.

Let's first consider each of the two classes: there is a dominant or privileged class that *stands opposed* to a fundamental or popular class. They differ, notably, in that they relate differently to the dichotomy of market-organisation, on the basis of which they are defined. The first contains two 'poles' that are marked by the privileges they respectively hold: *property* (on the market) and *competency* (concerning the means and ends of social organisation). These two sorts of power relation (connected to the two 'mediations') are exercised conjointly but unequally over the *entirety* of the fundamental class. This latter tends *therefore* to articulate itself not in two parts but in three 'fractions', in accordance with the prevalent mode of social coordination: depending on whether one is caught more in relations of organisation (e.g. functionaries) or in market relations (e.g. individual producers, or better, 'merchants') or instead in the intersection of the two (private sector wage earners). Both classes are therefore differently structured. The dominant class, small in number, comprises two social forces that oscillate between convergence and divergence. The other class, great in number, can only assert itself as such in a dialectic between the search for *unity* between its fractions and that for an *alliance* with knowledge-power – an alliance founded on the fact that the two factors of class do not present the same social properties. These diverse articulations, by which 'classes' *exist* – as disparate and fluid entities – only appear at a high cost, both theoretical (research in the social sciences) and practical (class struggle).

As to the two poles of the privileged class, the dissimilarity between them is just as great. Their mode of reproduction distinguishes them radically (see Marx on the former, and Bourdieu on the latter). The pole of capitalists, although eminently disparate, possesses a sort of systematic unity from the fact of its permanent reaffirmation through the process of capital accumulation, which links together all the actors involved in capitalist rivalry. It finds itself united under the hegemony of finance, as a concentrated and identifiable summit. The other pole – beyond the subdivision, which is a problematic continuum as well, between leaders and experts (analysed at §2.2.3 above) – only exists in the variety of functions of management and competency that the social dynamic calls for at each instant, and sees itself gathered together only through historically variable, strategic processes. Competent-elites perform only by being dispersed, by being distributed over incomparable sites, which cover diverse tasks that fall to individuals invested with competency to do. This competency affects individuals in their concrete – economic, familial, sexual ... – lives, that is, it affects subjects who are singular, educated, managed, apprehended, interpellated, cared for, administrated. It asserts itself through the relevant ruling bodies. But in these diverse functions, the great mass of 'competent' agents fall under the status of 'governed' more than of 'governors', in accordance with a continuum from one class to the other.

Lastly, concerning the fundamental or popular class, its unity is not immediately given either. This is, moreover, generally why we speak of the 'popular classes' – an epistemological obstacle masking their prospects of political unity. Here it is important to take various factors of division and dispersion into account.[5] The first thing requiring examination, however, falls under a principle of subdivision (*fractionnement*). Experience tells us today that, for a generation in its 'popular' mass, the entry into 'active life' – to the extent it is actually possible – contains three structurally distinct possibilities (albeit often more or less intertwined): to find a public sector or private sector job, or to become 'independently' self-employed (or supposedly so). But in order to establish that all three together configure a single class, in which the excluded themselves are stakeholders, a metastructural analysis is required to relate these diverse situations to the various compositions of market and organisational factors, to the variously balanced

---

[5] My argument here is cast in the abstract framework of class structures and it does not yet include the *other dimension* of the modern form of society, namely that of world-system, including its determinations of slavery, migration, racism and so on; nor, for that matter, does it yet include the *other* primary *social relationship,* which is to say the sexual relationship.

relations between the two 'mediations'. The mechanisms of exclusion, in their violence and radicality, ensue themselves from the perverse potentials specific both to the market and to organisation in the conditions of modern class relations – I will return to this.[6]

In sum, under these conditions there exists no absolute discontinuity between these classes, any more than between the poles of the dominant class. The petty capitalist also attends to management. And he is close to common people. This may also be true of managers and above all the agents of competency. The *division* is nonetheless essential. But it is to be taken in an active sense: not as a division but as a divisor. It does not furnish the principle of a tableau that would make it possible a priori to say where, among the population of functionaries, liberal professions and intellectual workers, one could establish a definite and stable limit between the dominant and the dominated: it separates classes through the *dynamic* that it generates. But this is also the way it unites. Created by class division, 'classes' exist as fluctuating groupings, or historical actors.

The situation is always shifting, and at each moment one can only seek to know who are one's friends, who one's enemies, one's partners, by considering the existing interrelation between the three 'social forces' – a task that falls to a metastructural theory of hegemony.

---

6 Metastructural analysis does not forget that these class relations are always entwined with gender relations. See below at §3.3.1.2.

In short, 'there are classes' – and I have tried to clarify the meaning of the expression. But it further remains to show that, if 'class' is only made up of singular exceptions, this is not only because individuals have a fluctuating and often uncertain relation to it. It is because the class *relationship* is itself made up of inter-individual *relations*. The metastructural approach – which can only be legitimated, to repeat, by the effects of knowledge that it generates and the horizon that it thus opens for practice – analyses the modern class structure as an 'instrumentalisation of reason'. It begins with the two rational mediations (market and organisation – the two modes of rational coordination *between* individuals at the social scale), each of which defines one of the two complementary 'poles' of our social 'reason'. Both these *inter-individual* mediations, by which these two social powers are implemented (as property-power and knowledge-power), constitute class *factors*, which combine to form the modern class *relationship*. *Inter-individuality is therefore constitutive of the concept of class.* This latter defines the conditions in which *individuals* – and not families, parents, villages or clans – buy, sell, employ, dismiss, judge, order, teach, cure but also contract, work, obey, resist, act as entrepreneurs, interpret, group together or divide into separate groups ('moral persons' only exist as such as an outcome of the market, organisational and discursive relations extant between individuals). This is the sense in which the 'modern class *relationship*' exists only via '(inter-individual) class *relations*'. But correlatively – insofar as the *class relationship* therefore only subsists in class *relations*

– each individual act (or act that marshals individuals) of work, obedience, reinterpretation, resistance, grouping, takes on a structural value, that is to say, concerns class and society as a whole. Each individual is a 'gesture' or 'act', in Yves Citton's sense,[7] being that which constitutes a sign for all within the overarching social confrontation. But it exists as such only because the aspect of collective structure is already there.

We struggle to grasp the relation between all these terms, the multiple relationships between individual and class. We struggle to catch sight of the important structural dimension of the class 'act' (*geste*) in a modest action from below; and yet, when 'the masses' are able to recognise themselves in it, this 'modest act' may work to displace class division (a woman throws herself out the window due to overwhelming pressure from the bank; people become indignant; finance retreats). We struggle to see the power of *class* in the inter-individual practices of competent agents, who exercise *their* jobs in the name of *their* superior knowledge; however, the competent agent gets his authority (his recognised competency) from a structural organisation and not from himself, and through its very exercise a class privilege is reproduced. Just as much do we struggle, conversely, to see *the individual* in the aggregation of proprietor-power in an anonymous society; and yet, behind shares there is the shareholder, as well as those who are at the disposal of his power, as we see in company closures. Behind the 'markets', that epistemological monster by whose name

7 Yves Citton, *Renverser l'insoutenable,* Paris: Seuil, 2012.

capitalist domination goes, it is necessary to identify the very concrete and powerfully organised individuals and groups bent on imposing their law.

In short, one cannot be both nominalist and structuralist without articulating the class *relationship* (rapport) together with the class *relation* (relation). And this presumes that we grasp the class *relationship* on the basis of both *class factors,* on the basis of both *instrumentalised inter-individual relations,* market and organisation, which constitute our reason itself in its common exercise.[8]

3.1.3 The micro-macrological articulation of the state

If things are this way for the state too, this is because the state itself is a class *relationship*: it partakes in the class *relationship* that structures society as a whole. This is true for Marx, but for also Foucault, as we shall see. Some points of clarification are nonetheless necessary before we arrive at the point where structuralism and nominalism can be articulated in a dialectic.

---

[8] Balibar rightly concludes the necessity of conceiving class relations in terms of relations between concrete individuals. See his 'Foucault and Marx: The question of nominalism', in *Michel Foucault, philosopher,* trans. and ed. Timothy J. Armstrong, London: Harvester Wheatsheaf, 1992, pp. 38–55. According to the metastructural analysis that I advance, to go from one level to the other, from the individual relationship to the general relation, and vice versa, both 'mediations' have to be considered, both inter-individual operators, which, as such, concern bodies: bodies in market transactions, bodies in organisation, continually normalised through power-knowledge – since, in modern society, market power is never applied outside of an organisation, outside a form of power-knowledge.

1. In this regard, 'power' in Foucault presents two inter-related traits: (a) first, it is a relationship between individuals; and (b) it is immanent to the set of social relationships. Both these statements are explicitly directed against Marx's approach, or at least against a run-of-the-mill Marxism.

(a) *Nominalism, at least to begin with* ... For, 'one probably ought to be nominalist'. Foucault clarifies this notably in the section on 'Method' in the *The History of Sexuality*.[9] Power, indeed, 'comes from everywhere', from a 'multitude of relations of force', and not from any 'central point', any radiating 'centre', any 'sovereignty', from 'the law' or from a 'headquarters', or from a 'group' controlling the apparatus. The state is nothing other than the 'institutional integration of power relations'. In this forest of metaphors, one thing should hold our Foucauldian-Marxian attention: a common recourse to an 'order of reasons', which is presented according to the schema of a 'before' and an 'after' and indicates what we must start and finish with. We have, 'to begin with', always specific force relations with no 'primary' central point; then, we 'ultimately arrive at overarching apparatuses', which result from the 'integration' of particular powers. There is a necessary order to the account: nothing about the *whole* can be said before the elements of which it is the amalgamation are revealed. This order of reasons imposes itself upon the theoretician: as regards social ontology, there have to be a set of *raisons d'être*.

---

9 Foucault, *History of Sexuality,* Vol.1, pp. 92–102.

However, the account in *Capital,* we ought not forget, proceeds in similar fashion. Rigorously speaking, Marx cannot *start* with the class relationship (or with the class state). For him, nothing can be said about capital, which is a structural concept, prior to having recognised the market, a nominalist concept, in which only individuals are recognised. In Section 1, there exist only relations between individuals in a market logic of production (see §1.1.2 above). And Marx's problem is precisely to find the theoretical path that leads us *from the relation* between individuals on the market *to the capitalist class relationship.* The question that Marx and Foucault each ask is thus one and the same: how it is possible to be both structuralist and nominalist? Or rather, such is the question we face and are obliged to answer.

(b) *The immanence of 'power' to the set of social relations.*

There is a sort of schematism [says Foucault] 'that needs to be avoided here – and which is incidentally not to be found in Marx – that consists in locating power in the state apparatus, and in making the state apparatus the major, privileged, capital and almost unique instrument of the power of one class over another. In reality, power in its exercise goes much further, passes through much finer channels, and is much more ambiguous, since at bottom each individual is nominally the bearer of a power, and to this extent, can convey power. Power does not have as its sole function to reproduce the relations of production. The networks of domination and the circuits of exploitations interact, intersect and support each other, but they do not coincide (*PK*/72; tm).

Several themes converge here. Immanence is not about coincidence, but instead about overlapping and crosschecking. Let's bear in mind that 'power relations are not in a position of exteriority as regards other types of relations (economic production, relations of knowledge, sexual relations) but are immanent to them'. Foucault conceives class power and state power in the dispersion of multiple mechanisms of power. He assents ('absolutely', he says) to the suggestion of Michèle Perrot: 'you are opposed to the idea of power as a superstructure, but not to the idea that power is in some sense consubstantial with the development of productive forces' (*PK*/159).

2. But when Marxism refuses to see in the state an institution existing above classes, above a 'civil society' (to put it in the liberal idiom), when Marxism turns it into a 'matter of class', and when it thus distinguishes 'state' and 'state apparatus' in the narrow sense, it is very precisely this idea that is introduced: that the state is immanent to all social relations insofar as they are relationships of class. The superstructure is immanent to the base. Its (class) power is exercised in this inter-individuality, which is that of (inter-individual) class relations as implied in the class relationship. This is why the 'impersonality' of modern social relations is wholly relative. In short, there is no opposing Foucault and Marx on these grounds. Everything is political, up to and including inter-individuality: this is something they each show in their own way.

One can, in actual fact, just as easily place them back to back. But it cannot be done using the same terms. Foucault, it has been said, sought to restrict his programme. His nominalism is also a pretext not to have to contend with the being of structures and totalities. He relies on what has already been said before him about classes (and, in this sense at least, about the state *qua* class state): he speaks of them as things that everyone knows about, and therefore, but in a weak sense, this is not his problem. What he essentially says is, 'Of course structures exist in the background, but I'm going to talk to you about something else.'[10] And it might be thought that he was perfectly right in doing so. He followed his own genius: he opened *another site,* another 'continent', and showed that he had an immense amount to teach us. His discoveries have rebounded onto the Marxian site, that of the structures and ensembles it defines. Marx also sought to tackle this nominalism/structuralism dilemma. But he seems not to have led his research through to its end. I will therefore try to press on further with it.

3. It is only in their *dialectic* that the 'relation' and the 'relationship' can only be thought together. This is precisely what meta/structural research strives to do (where the '/' designates the dialectical relation between both terms: metastructure

---

[10] On the variety of formulations – 'hegemony', 'supremacy', 'surplus power', etc. – through which the processes of global forms of domination are evoked, see Bob Jessop, 'Pouvoir et strategie chez Poulantzas et Foucault', *Marx et Foucault, Actuel Marx, No. 36,* Paris: PUF, 2004, p. 101. They do not aim to *conceptualise* this globality as such.

and structure). And, as we have seen, this attempt takes its inspiration from Marx's schema in *Capital* (despite its flawed 'unipolarity' – for, as I've tried to show, it is centred on the inter-individual aspect of the market and cut off from the 'between-all' aspect of organisation). The order of the Marxian account has not pedagogical but rather theoretical reasons: it governs a project of social ontology. And it moves from the relation to the relationship and then from the relationship to the relation, its aim being to understand modern society as a process, a process that, however, is not a functionalism.

(a) There is indeed a nominalist beginning, one that reduces every debate to what is and what must be: one in which each person is defined as a free interlocutor equal to all others. Marx describes it, in Section 1, as the world of the modern (amphibological) claim: ours is a market society, a totality made up of individuals who deem themselves free and able to exchange their services, their work, in the form of commodities (goods or services). What we have here is a presumed *relation*, a 'metastructure'.

(b) In fact, in Section 3 we learn the following: this presumed free-market *relation* is in fact posited, generated, by the modern class *relationship* (or: the metastructure posited, generated by class structure, which commodifies labour power). But, by positing the social body as a set of free and rational individuals, this class relationship splits it into two classes: there are those who possess the means of production and there are wage-earning labourers who, in selling their labour power, produce. Through exploitation what thus comes to be reproduced is a totality of class. What we have here is the *relationship* actualised, that is, the 'structure'.

(c) But the implementation of this class *relationship* is accounted for in terms of class *relations*. Each capitalist only accomplishes himself as such in his relation of competition with other capitalists, whom he must keep outdoing. Each wage earner is in rivalry with other wage earners, since at each moment the threat looms of being replaced by someone better able to execute the business of profit making. Both classes are also realised in the inter-individual aspect; that is, as the singular couple (employer/employee) engaging in contractual relations. This is at least 'initially' so, for here is where the classes clash in their presence, or at least the groups that they create, under the conditions defined by the class *relationship*. Under these conditions, it is *individuals* who struggle, who interpret situations, weigh up the pros and cons and engage each other. 'Practices'.

(a-b-c) It is here that the *social dialectic* resides, i.e. in this unity of the class 'relationship–relation'. One is always referred back to the inter-individual *relation* of one to one and between all. But it is the class *relationship* that refers us to it. As Marx explains, the capitalist class *relationship* is what generates the market relationship as universal. More precisely, class *structure* defines the contradictory field of economic *practices* (which are also social and political) that are possible within the modern form of society. These practices 'posit' the *metastructure*. This is because they are always at the same time *speech acts*. At each moment the metastructural presupposition can thereby find itself recast in its substantial content; that is, in the meaning given to freedom and equality and the status conferred on rationality (the free disposal of one's body or freedom of expression, recognised access to the resources of knowledge, and so on to infinity). The class *relationship,* as a division that is always differently reproduced, is thus in perpetual movement, always opening up other fields of possible practice.

4. It is in these terms that we are to understand the *state.* As Foucault puts it, 'The state does not have an essence. [It] is nothing else than the mobile effect of a regime of multiple governmentalities' *(BB/*77). This non-essentiality, this mobility, this movement, comes to light in dialectical terms.

(a) *The metastructural state* is the state considered abstractly as 'prior to classes'.[11] It is the *state that is proclaimed* in the

---

[11] The presentation of *Capital* unfolds according to three levels of abstraction: if we call N1 the register of general anthropological concepts, such as that of work in general, we must then distinguish between levels N2, which is that of market relations of productions in general, and N3, which is that of properly capitalist relations. In Section 1 of *Capital,* Marx provides an outline of a theory of the 'metastructural State', in which capitalist society is grasped at the level N2: that is, *before* level N3 of the class relationship. It is this 'before' in the theoretico-logical sense that is proper to the metastructure. That is, this before is the moment when work is not yet considered waged (but only as producing commodities), nor the market as capitalist. Nor the state as a class state. And yet, as Marx insists here, the state is already there, implied both in money and in the presumed given of territory. In Chapter 3 of *Théorie générale,* I take up this essential analysis, curiously ignored by the Marxist tradition, which thus fails to reach a dialectical conception (a meta/structural one) of the modern form of society, despite it being sketched in this important work. [Trans. – For a more detailed presentation of this formalisation of Marx's account, the reader may refer to the article in which Bidet first presented it, 'Misère dans la philosophie marxiste: Moishe Postone lecteur du Capital', in *Périodes,* November 2014. He reprises this formalisation in *Le Sujet interpellé et le corps biopolitique* (forthcoming).]

constitutional definition that it gives of itself, which one finds constantly reiterated in public discourse. *It is, at least supposedly, pure civic organisation,* a pure organisation of speech, founded on the axiom 'one voice = one voice' and on the 'metastructural asymmetry' that at this level of principle rejects the market relation as 'corruption'. It *supposedly* governs the set of *presumed* institutions necessary for the elaboration and implementation of common laws and decisions. *The declared state is not nothing.* Class structure is both hidden and revealed within it. Class structure comes to be 'heard' in this state through the *amphibology* of a shared declaration, one voiced by those up above who state that this proclaimed order has been achieved and by those down below who retort that it is still to come. It is an *amphibological* declaration since all involved nonetheless continue to fly the same flag of liberty-equality-rationality. It is this 'essentially contested concept'[12] that defines the metastructure. This is also to say that this concept *is* a challenge, and hence a stake.

(b) *The structural state* is the state in its effectivity as the modern class state, the 'presupposition' of which is the metastructural declaration of freedom, equality and rational relations between individuals. This state exerts a class power that produces class confrontation, the outcome of which

---

[12] Here I adopt a concept introduced by Walter Brice Gallie, which also expresses the French term *'différend'* (disagreement, difference of opinion) in a way that makes it useful for a theory of modernity. That is the aim of chapter 6 of *L'État-monde,* 'Idéologies, utopies et cryptologies', the idea being that the modern nation-state process encloses all citizens in the same conceptual constraint. This is what a metastructural theory of the above-mentioned 'essentially contested concept' strives to explain.

depends on the force relations that obtain in the social, economic and cultural fabric, in the conjuncture and over the long term. The designation 'dominant class', which suggests that the entire social domain flows from its domination, does not tell us everything about the class relationship. It is not valid to attribute to the 'power of the bourgeoisie' everything that appears (schools, hospitals, social laws, political freedoms) in the course of it supposedly being 'in power'. It remains for us to analyse what it is that the creative power of the popular class consists (see below at §4.1.2).

(c) *The concrete state* is a process that unfolds, through *practices,* in *the relation between metastructure and structure.* The antagonistic economic, cultural and political practices of individuals and groups, intervening in a war of position between classes, work continually to shake up – at the same time as the *structural* front line: unity or dispersion, reversal of alliances, advances or withdrawals on the path to emancipation – the content of what comes to be (contradictorily) declared in *metastructural* fashion.

Thus understood, the dialectic is the real form of relation between realities that nominalism and structuralism each grasp one-sidedly. By inscribing Foucault's nominalism within this structural-dialectical framework, historical thoroughness can be maintained. For the singularity of the individual relates no longer to an essence, but instead to an uncertainty – which plays out in shifting spaces, shifting yet nevertheless strictly mapped – of class structures, which have their own dynamic, itself always already uncertain.

3.2 APPARATUSES OF POWER
VERSUS CLASS STRUCTURES

Marx theorised what could be designated as social 'apparatuses'. Foucault never fails to relate his analyses to a 'class' society. The one, however, focuses on the *class structure* and its revolutionary historical potential; the other, on the *apparatuses of power* that unfold as grand strategies. Foucault does not propose, properly speaking, a general theory of modern history to rival Marx's. However, the dichotomy apparatus/strategy does express a set of inquiries into the limits of the Marxian perspective. It illustrates the well-foundedness of taking a nominalist approach to historical processes, understood as involving, at each moment, a multitude of nerve centres and objects that are irreducible in cause, scale and temporality to one another (§3.2.1). But can it be said that the Foucauldian critique thus works to render vain the revolutionary ambition, expressed by Marx in structural terms, to *abolish* class structure? (§3.2.2).

3.2.1 Foucault: strategies in relation
to 'apparatuses of power'

The Archaeology of Knowledge brought to light 'discursive formations', defined as 'sets of practices that systematically form the objects of which they speak'. It welcomed them in their fundamental dispersion and not by derivation on the basis of any era-specific 'vision of the world'[13] or of a rationality

---

[13] 'A world-view'. Michel Foucault, *The Archaeology of Knowledge & The Discourse on Language*, trans. A. M. Sheridan Smith, London: Tavistock Publications, 1972, p. 69.

that would progressively affirm itself in history. It nonetheless discovered in them an 'episteme', a general apparatus, but as yet a 'specifically discursive' one (*PK*/197), which made it possible to establish within a field of scientificity what can be qualified as scientific and what not.

As it appeared in his later work, the concept of 'apparatus' comes to embrace 'the entire field of the non-discursive social' (*PK*/198). A broader concept then emerged that designated, on each occasion, a heterogeneous network of discourses, institutions, law, architecture, etc. (*PK*/196).[14] Foucault gives as an example of an 'apparatus' that which presided over strategies to settle the working population in the northern and eastern areas of France in the nineteenth century. Not only were these populations to be supplied with lodgings, credit, grocery stores and savings banks but discourses of philanthropy, unionism, patrons, education, etc, also arose (*PK*/202–3). The Council of Trent (*PK*/200) is another example, as it formed the basis on which a whole ensemble of micro-relations developed around the guidance of consciousness, confession, in short, a new subjectivity. Eighteenth-century health polices provide yet another example: they formed 'an apparatus that would ensure not only [the population's] 'subjection' [*assujetissement*] but the constant increase of its utility' (*EWF3*/96). Foucault can

---

14 Foucault explains this concept in various places. See notably his interview given in 1977 and first published in French in *Ornicar?* (The English translation is to be found in *PK*/194-228). The interest of the interview resides notably in the quality and the acuity of the questioning of his interlocutors.

speak just as easily of apparatuses of psychiatry or of sexuality (in order: the ancient apparatus of pleasures, the Christian apparatus of the flesh, the modern one of sex), etc., and an apparatus can further be 'an army or a workshop, or some other such type of institution' (*PK*/159; tm).

If everything, if the social as a whole, is thus an 'apparatus', then what definite meaning does this latter term have? To which definite intention does it correspond? The notion of 'apparatus' is regularly directed against two adversaries: against a liberalism that would derive power from a purported power of sovereignty, of legislation, of the constitution; and against a Marxism presumed to conceive of this in terms of the state, or state apparatus (*appareil*) (*DE3*/201). By contrast, what each of these more or less fictive foils legitimates is a realist approach that consists in grasping all social institutions as 'apparatuses' (*dispositifs*): that is to say, as relations of power, which is always the power of some over others, in the concreteness of 'technologies', material assemblages and discursive formations. In modern times, we move towards a biopolitics of populations (we return to these concepts in the following chapter), according to dynamics both of domination and promotion. Such a definition of apparatus, however, says nothing about the problems it bears within.

In fact, to talk of 'apparatuses' is not merely to evoke a *factual arrangement*, a simple configuration of places, discourse, spaces, times ... It is also presented here, somewhat surreptitiously, as a teleological concept, since it presumes an agency that *arranges* with a view to certain ends. But which agency is this? It is not

Reason in history: Foucault does not defend another 'invisible hand'. Instead, as he says, 'I think one needs to look at how the great strategies of power encrust themselves and find their conditions of exercise in micro-relations of power' (*PK*/199; tm). But, we might ask, in accordance with which relation between the micro and the macro does this happen? Which relation between tactics and strategy? Strategies are the result of tactics, of which they ceaselessly redefine the framework. This is how things transpire with the patronal apparatus in northern France in the nineteenth century: ultimately, 'one *obtains* (my emphasis) a coherent, rational overall strategy but one of which is it impossible to say who conceived it' (*PK*/203). This is the meaning of Foucault's statement that we are dealing with 'strategies without a strategist'. But this amounts only to the formulation of a problem. For, how does 'one obtain' (and who is this 'one'?) a strategy on the basis of a sum of tactics?

Here we delve further into the issue at hand, since it is apparent that Foucault has in view, specifically, and problematically, the emergence of 'class strategies'. Apparatuses, implemented on the basis of multiple small powers, form the sites where 'tactics' can be observed, and which 'take shape in piecemeal fashion, before a class solidifies them into vast coherent ensembles (*PK*/159; tm). 'One can even say that this is the strategy that allows the bourgeois class to be the bourgeois class and to exercise its domination. But what I don't think one can say is that it's the bourgeois class on the level of its ideology or its economic project that, as a sort of at once real and fictive subject, invented and forcibly imposed this strategy on the working class' (*PK*/203). Thus conceived, strategy forms class (as Althusser says: class struggle precedes classes). But it does not constitute it as *subject*. This is the crucial point here.

To the question 'But then what role does social class play?' Foucault replies: 'Ah, here we are at the centre of the problem, and no doubt also of the obscurities of my own discourse. A dominant class isn't a mere abstraction, but neither is it a pre-given entity. For a class to become a dominant class, for it to ensure its domination and for that domination to reproduce itself is certainly the effect of a number of actual pre-meditated tactics operating within the grand strategies that ensure this domination' (*PK*/203).[15] In short, social class is indeed something real: 'it is not an abstraction'. This totality certainly pertains to a social ontology. But it is not 'pre-given'; 'it is produced'. We are still within the metaphor of 'before and after': we must *begin* with tactics in order adequately to be able to conceive of class-forming strategies, because this is how things proceed in reality.

But which is the reality at stake here? For it remains to be known which status Foucault gives to the concept of 'class', a concept he uses frequently. Significantly, 'class' does not feature in the glossary of *Dits et Écrits*, which suggests that

---

[15] The theme of 'class struggle', it will be noted, is recurrent in Foucault until such time as his interest begins to turn toward liberalism. See his dialogue in 1978 with Marxist dissident Ryumei Yoshimoto on the topic of 'how to rid oneself of Marxism': 'Marx effectively says that class struggle is the motor of history. [...] Indeed, it's an undeniable fact.' But, he adds, 'what is struggle?' And for starters 'who enters into the struggle?' and so on (*DE3*/606).

there is no specifically Foucauldian meaning to be found in it. This term in effect functions in his discourse in a sense that is presumed to be accepted, with a semantic charge, now economic, now political, that he certainly seems to get from the Marxist tradition. On the other hand, however, Foucault provides a *critique* of the concept of class, which amounts to proposing a new version of it: not to make it disappear from the theoretical field, but, in the fashion of analytic Marxists, to conceive of class on the basis of singular relations. Foucault makes use of a (weak) holism, which is critically conceived on the basis of a (strong) in-principle nominalism.

But this sequence – from the 'relation' to the 'relationship' – does not appear to be taken up with the consistency that one would expect. Jacques Rancière (*PK*/141–2) suggests that if 'class struggle' is not the '*ratio* for the exercise of power', it nonetheless functions as a 'final guarantee of intelligibility of techniques for the dressage of body and mind (the production of a labour force suitable for the tasks assigned to it by capitalist exploitation, and so forth)'. Foucault replies that this is indeed right. This is not to say that the disciplines work in the service of a supposedly primitive 'economic interest', but instead that they 'can be used in strategies'. 'Class struggle can therefore not be "the *ratio* for the exercise of power" and nonetheless be the "guarantee of intelligibility" of certain grand strategies'. We cannot fail to notice here that the 'final guarantee of intelligibility' strongly resembles the concept of the 'last instance', which defines a very real object. A final instance of intelligibility: on this basis (or by returning to it –

another metaphor) one can understand what sorts of singular things and facts can come about.

For, these tactics, from which a strategy will emerge, certainly also appear in Foucault *to proceed* from interests or from preoccupations *of class*. Hence, concerning the paternalist patronat of the nineteenth century: the strategy of 'moralisation of the working class' 'was accomplished because it met the urgent need to master a vagabond, floating labour force' (*PK*/204). Similarly with the 'example' of the 'medico-legal apparatus of psychiatry': here, it is not the word 'urgency' that suits, but that of the 'necessity' for psychiatrists to have themselves recognised as elements of public hygiene and to be seen as vital for the magistrates (*PK*/205). This is a class concern, one specific, this time, to the 'competent-elites'.

In sum, Foucault is set within contradictory constraints. On the one hand, he has to hold firm to some sort of nominalism, which he views as a guarantee against every 'philosophy of history' and, on the other, he has to conceptualise the great ensembles and their overall movements. Lastly, in the nine-teenth century, he says, 'bourgeois power' was 'able to elaborate grand strategies, without one needing for all that to impute a subject to them (*PK*/207). Thus, to Alain Grosrichard, who reminds him of the Marxists' question, 'Who are our friends, who are our enemies?' (*PK*/208), he replies: 'I would say it's all against all. There aren't immediately given subjects of the struggle, one the proletariat, the other the bourgeoisie.' He is of course prompted to say that what prevails is 'a mess', the general disorder of battle. But we must ultimately ask how some come to win over others: we must 'pose the problem in terms of strategy' (*PK*/209). In terms of class strategy. In terms of class.

To recapitulate: class logic is not primary, but rather the 'ultimate guarantee of intelligibility'. In order properly to understand the situation, we have to set out from it once more. The thousand and one tactics that we see at work are not *deducible* from the strategic imperatives of class: they are utilised by them. But they ultimately *converge* in grand strategies, which form the context of their reiteration. So we end up with a sort of circular relation between the individual moment and the structural moment, something that one finds in diverse forms in all sociological reflection. Foucault arranges the battlefield by defining as primary the moment of the particular, construed in terms of 'tactic', and as secondary the overall movement, conceived in terms of strategy. But this language game does not manage to exorcise the phantom of the 'dominant class', which he cannot fail to mention again and again, in its strategic existence – an identification of actions and individual passions.

As we've seen (§3.1.2), this is the circularity that the dialectic 'metastructure/structure/practices' seeks to account for, with reference to the conceptuality of the meta/structural first initiated by Marx. It nonetheless remains to find out if this 'meta-Marxist' problematic of 'structure' (defined in its relation between practices and metastructure) can embrace everything that is theoretically and politically heralded in the concept of 'apparatus'. This might indicate that a 'structural' problematic is not enough to devise the programme of a politics of emancipation. We will come to this in §3.3 below. To see things more clearly, however, it is first necessary to consider where things are with Marxian 'structure' and the 'reconstructive' critique to which it must be submitted.

3.2.2 Marx: strategies in relation to 'class structures'

If it is difficult to contrast Foucault and Marx here, the reason is that the one grasps things in terms of 'apparatuses', the other in terms of 'structures'. In a conceptuality inherited from Marx, Foucauldian 'apparatuses' seem to have to be conceived on the basis of 'structures' (of class and in a context that is 'systemic' – in the sense of a 'world-system'). But if we are to understand the strategies and tactics deployed in them, and notably those that Foucault taught us to recognise, a recasting of the Marxian framework is in my view necessary, one that inscribes the capitalist structure defined by Marx in the 'metastructural' framework pertaining to the modern form of society. It is necessary to refound, broaden and redialecticise Marx's structuralism. But the terms of this task are still unclear.

The temporality involved in each of the concepts of apparatus and structure is not the same. An 'apparatus', as a confrontation of force relations, raises the problem of its continued existence. And this is because it is understood as an apparatus of *power,* in Foucault's sense (see *DE4*/241). Power is always *faced:* it encounters resistances. It seeks to maintain and develop itself as power. It does not seek a 'victory' that would neutralise the given partner, but rather to assert itself as such, as a power over this latter, as a power to direct. It endures as a form of unstable stability. 'In fact, between relationships of power and strategies of struggle there is a reciprocal appeal, a continual linking and a perpetual reversal' (*EWF3*/347). Eternal return? The same historical events can be read as power and as struggle, because struggle and power intermingle. One is thus returned to the relative *stability* of an unequal force relation between those who *exercise* it and those that *resist* it. 'Domination', which, says Foucault, 'marks a large part of the history of humanity', is this very intermingling. It is the transformation of one into another. The one's supporting the other. This does not take place, he specifies, in the sense of an organic equilibrium: 'in order for a certain relation of forces not to maintain itself but to accentuate, stabilise and broaden itself, a certain kind of manoeuvre is necessary' (*PK*/206). In short, what tactics and strategies for domination seek is the continued existence and development of apparatuses of power.

'Structure' presents a wholly other problem: that of its *reproduction*. Foucault's formulation here may appear close to Marx's, according to which the history of humanity is from the beginning 'the history of class struggle'. But if, with Marx, this class confrontation possesses a long-term *stability*, this is not because power and struggle summon one another in 'endless linkings and perpetual reversals', and thus in some sense by creating an equilibrium. It is because the specificity of class structure, and specifically of the capitalist structure of production, consists in its containing the immanent conditions of its *reproduction*. The theme of apparatuses, strategies and tactics that Foucault brings to light with such blinding clarity hides the absence of a category that is required here: that of structure. The Foucauldian 'apparatus', as an *overarching* mechanism, which gives rise to great strategies of power, tends to occupy the function belonging to structure. If it is not suitable for filling this function this is because in itself it does not possess a property that is inherent to 'structure', which is to *reproduce itself*. The concept of structure thus responds to the question implicitly raised in Foucault's statement that class 'is not an abstraction'. Class structure is the *real* context of a set of practices *in actu*. If it has no place, except trivial (non-productive), in the form of a nominalist ontology such as Foucault's, this is because the latter – in contrast with what we see in Bourdieu – has no problematic of 'reproduction': of *structural* reproduction. Let us first consider the analysis of his historical movement. Both in Marx and in Foucault the same reference can be found to what could be called a 'strategic cohesion': the working class, the industrial patronat, the hospital body, the Tridentine Church, etc. But Foucault considers common strategies on the basis of concrete tactics that converge on one another, while Marx researches the structural conditions of the very existence of these strategies, that is to say, of the social forces that intervene in history. The structures that he constructs theoretically are more abstract realities than strategies: they are the divisions that *give rise* to the latter. Marx argues on the basis of structure: if such-and-such a capitalist fails to reproduce himself as such, the structure will reproduce itself all the same. Marx is thus led to focus on the *proper being of structures,* that is on the principles of their movements: on the one hand, of their reproduction, on the other, of the transformations that flow from their structural configuration, that is to say, at once from their productivity and from their contradictions. According to his view, the capitalist structure, founded on wage labour exploitation in a context of competition to maximise surplus value, necessarily evolves towards an industrial concentration of capital, which ultimately generates, at least potentially, its own 'gravedigger'. It is in this context that the overarching strategies, fed by day-to-day tactics, come to clash. Later Marxism exists only insofar as it conserves this paradigm of 'structure/reproduction/tendency', even if this means inflecting it in diverse ways. The Foucauldian approach in terms of 'apparatuses' attests to a similar ambition: to interpret the world with the aim of transforming it. Or at least with the aim of improving it in some fashion.[16] But the 'apparatuses' of power it makes appear belong to a context of tendencies that they cannot explain of themselves. Indeed, one cannot risk the diagnosis of a historical *tendency* – which does not imply any teleological perspective – along with its possible counter-tendencies, except within the consideration of a determinate *structure*; that is, by seeking to clarify its tendential properties. It is not to be forgotten that

---

[16] See especially his interview from 1983, 'Structuralism and Poststructuralism', with Gérard Raulet, *EWF2*/433–58. In it he says, 'the task of philosophy is to say what today is' and to say what 'we are today', to decipher, via the 'network of contingencies' how things 'have been made' and how they can 'be unmade' (pp. 449–50).

singular conjunctures always occur at the juncture of multiple tendential phenomena. But it is still necessary for the said social structure to be correctly established, above all if the issue is to think up a strategy with the aim of abolishing it. Foucault's shortcomings do not ensure Marx's pertinence. What must we change in these two bodies of thought, then, to enable them to join together in a common programme of critical analysis oriented around a horizon of emancipation?

In coming to this question, I ask myself, however, if the 'lack' with which I have hitherto charged Foucault is not the underside of a certain 'pertinence'.

This would indeed explain why – to the great astonishment of some of Marx's disciples, convinced that his theory possesses sufficient heuristic and political value in all registers of the social order – so much research and so many struggles have found their standard-bearer in Foucault, and in fields where Marxism seems able to intervene only after the fact, a position that, not being hegemonic, is rather uncomfortable for it. To grasp this, I now take up the problem again at a further remove from each of them.

3.3 SHORTCOMINGS AND RELEVANCE OF MARX AND FOUCAULT

Thus far we have considered Marx and Foucault as though they reflected each other in a mirror, summoning each to find himself in the world of the other. This exercise has its limits. Marx's conceptuality has a determinate object, which we shall provisionally call 'capitalism' – the capitalist class *relationship*. Foucault has a larger embrace: class, but also *sex* (understood, it is true, as sexuality and not in the sense of gender relations). And this opens up other perspectives (§3.3.1). The difference of object is also indicated by the fact that Foucault challenges the problematic of class and state, grasped until now as marking the epicentre of Marxism, by bringing to light the disquieting paradigm of the 'war of races' as an 'analyser' of society. So, in addition to class and sex, we also have 'race'. Notwithstanding some gaps that will require identifying, this triptych seems utterly complete (§3.3.2).

But how can we conceive these three planks together? And how can we pull Marx and Foucault together? Is it possible to constitute a larger conceptual field that makes it possible to formulate the conditions of a politics in which each of them could recognise themselves (§3.3.3)?

3.3.1 Class, sex, race: a Foucauldian triptych?

From the 1970s on, Foucault engaged in a struggle around prisons. He played, along with others around him (Daniel Defert, J. M. Domenach, Pierre Vidal-Naquet and others), the role of initiator, establishing a programme of information in which those concerned could have their voices heard. And he inspired other initiatives of the same kind.[17] He also intervened

---

17 In the wake of the GIP, Group for Information on Prisons, came the GIA, Group for Information on Asylum, GITS, Group for Information on Social Workers, and GIS, Group for Information on Health. After Foucault's death in 1984, Daniel Defert established Aides, an association for fighting

regularly in the key questions raised by the 'new social movements'. The important thing here, more so than his own engagement, is the fact that these 'movements' immediately recognised themselves in his mode of analysis and critique, discovering in his 'box of tools' the conceptual instruments they had required and that, even in the eyes of those who continued to make reference to it, Marx's method could not provide for. Foucault's major historical and philosophical writings from the 1960s were received with fervour in major intellectual circles. The *History of Madness in the Classical Age* immediately earned him a large notoriety. But the works of the 1970s, carried by the wave of 1968, in which Foucault came to have a place, would also profoundly affect 'public opinion'. As we shall see, *Discipline and Punish*, from 1975, still belonged to a certain Marxist heritage. His own conceptual innovations, however, would destine him to go further. A great deal of his previous work had, to be sure, traversed objects and problems that were

---

AIDS. Such initiatives, it will be noted, nonetheless did not emerge from out of a politico-cultural desert. Foucault wrote that prior to the 1960s, Marxists and other 'people on the left' had considered 'problems of psychiatry and sexuality' as 'marginal and minor' (*DE3*/472–3). Nevertheless, we might mention, among others, the subversive initiatives undertaken in the 1940s in the field of 'institutional psychotherapy', from Saint-Alban to La Borde. These occurred against the backdrop of people having both Marxist and libertarian commitments, who were under the aegis of Marx and of Freud. We can name here, for instance, François Tosquelles, Jean Oury and Lucien Bonnafé, and later also Tony Lainé, the latter two being active members of the French Communist Party. This history is a complex one, but it might be deemed after the fact that the 'anti-alienist' movement, stimulated by the idea that psychiatric activity ought to be articulated together with social struggles, eventually thwarted the antagonisms that stood in its way, as the intersection of these various heritages attests.

not part of the great history of emancipation via a revolution in the relations of production. But the novel radicality of his thought and its subversive potential did not seem to surface in social space beyond traditionally politicised milieus until after his account of 'apparatuses of sex' in *The History of Sexuality* (1976), which, illuminating *après coup* his works on madness, the hospital, the school, the prison, justice, the asylum, and architecture, confirmed his status as a master thinker able to orient critique across the entire front of social functions and to inspire a vast field of research and of struggles in parallel.[18]

1. Why is it necessary to attribute such an important role to his works on sexuality?[19] This, it seems to me, is because they most clearly had the effect of disrupting the course of 'social science'. About sex, the other major theories seemed to have nothing *specific* to say. That is, unless we are talking about psychoanalysis, but the problem is precisely that psychoanalysis struggles to affirm itself as a *social* theory. Foucault for his part reproached it for being a purely ahistorical conceptual matrix.[20] As for Marxism, it relies on a

---

[18] In reference to Foucault, §3.3.1 takes up a set of ideas and hypotheses that are discussed and argued for in chapter 5 of *L'État-monde,* 'Classe, Race, Sexe'.

[19] On this point, once more see Balibar's article 'Foucault et Marx'. Echoes of this essay are to be found in the following pages.

[20] Contrary to Foucault's reading, Stéphane Haber analyses the impact of psychoanalysis on anthropology in *Freud et la théorie sociale* (Paris: La Dispute, 2012) and also shows, in his *Freud sociologue* (Paris: Le Bord de l'Eau, 2012), that it is possible to glean a genuine sociology from it, namely a 'sociology of the singular'. He argues that in the interwar period Freud actually recast psychoanalysis within a historical horizon.

well-circumscribed configuration of social relations: relations between work, means of production, modes of control, modes of appropriation, etc., along with their political, juridical, ideological conditions. It is unable to exit this circle, unless by crossing its conceptual figures with others *defined outside of it.* Historical and sociological research has obviously long been interested in the family, in gender relations and in sexuality. But Foucault disrupts disciplinary regions by introducing the concept of *power-knowledge,* which makes it possible to analyse 'sex' as an apparatus of social power correlated to a social knowledge. At issue here is a new universal operator that grasps power as close as possible to the social materiality of singular bodies and of a population of bodies, and that traverses the entire range of sexual life from the economy of pleasures to reproduction. The paradox is that Foucault, at this moment of his trajectory, continues strongly to anchor his research in the Marxist framework, as the chapter on the 'periodisation' of sexuality (*HS*, 115–31) attests. He sees in it 'the self-affirmation of one [class] rather than the subjugation of another', unless indirectly; that is to say, a concern with one class maintaining 'its differential value'. He describes a 'body of class', of 'sexualities of class', a sexuality that is 'originally, historically bourgeoise', and that, for hegemonic purposes, is exported to the proletariat. But the events he relates thus exceed the Marxian grand narrative, into which the 'hysterical woman' and the 'perverse adult' can only enter from the side. With the concept of knowledge-power, we are able to understand better (even if this is not Foucault's specific aim) that alongside social class relations *there are* also social relations of *sex,* which demand their own theorisation. Critical theory must consider such relations for themselves, without immediately neutralising them in class relations. In this way, it is possible to give consistency to the open and discontinuous field of all that exceeds the order of class. In contrast with Marx, he affirms another thought of the whole, thus providing another rallying point. Under the aegis of power-knowledge, Foucault discovers another continent: that of the treatment of individuals in their corporeal singularity, a treatment of people by people that is irreducible to a logic especially attributable to capital, and which traverses the entirety of the society. He 'liberates' us from Marxism.

Foucault took *sexuality* as his object. He did not push his investigation in the direction of 'gender relations', something that feminism has maintained is a shortcoming.

But feminist and homosexual militancy spontaneously recognised themselves in his discourse, which cleared another path of analysis for them than the one Marxism had opened. Despite all the disagreements, however, it would no doubt be better to bank on prospects for cooperation. Marx-inspired materialist feminism, at least in its most consequential versions, did not wait for Foucault to arrive before engaging in the study of 'social relations of sex'. This militant sociology brought to light two things: that these two sorts of social relations cross over and mutually condition each other (thus relations of sex are also, among others, relations of production), and that they are part of heterogeneous temporalities. The time of class can be accounted for on the basis of the relation *structure/ tendency* (to industrial concentration, to the wage-earning class's gaining in power ...), which is continuously disrupted in conjunctural fashion but is always resilient: it is a time oriented towards the revolution that has to *abolish* the class *relationship*. The relationship of sex knows of no such structure/tendency dichotomy, nor, therefore, does it have the same temporality, and nor is it oriented toward the same end. It maintains its own urgencies. It does not wait for the time of structure. It does not await the signs or the watchwords of the class relationship. It is necessary to define its specific grammar, which is not that of the 'mediations' of market/organisation, even if it is curbed by the terms of their instrumentalisation. It is the site of a relation of domination, and calls for a struggle that is focused, as Foucault says, on the 'immediate' enemy, not on the 'chief enemy' – this point is arguable. As Christine Delphy puts it: one identifies the latter in the former and is thus led to undertake autonomous combats. Alongside the common struggle that, placed on the agenda by the divulging of class relations, is oriented toward universal emancipation, there are thus combats that concern in a distinct way definite parts of the human community, of which 'minorities' – including the position of women relative to the whole of the social body, which they represent in equal part – seem paradoxically to provide the paradigm. Minorities have their own time, their own absolute urgency. They cannot be left to trail behind the class struggle, whether in theory or in practice. Class analysis, when carried out correctly, also helps us to understand that there are other social relations than those of class. And Foucault's lesson, which bears specifically on sexuality, is striking in this regard.

The 'minorities' are to be understood as in opposition not to a 'majority' but to a *totality,* a totality taken in its historical movement. They represent parts that do not have the status of being a *pars totalis* – that is to say a part expressing the whole – a notion that Althusser had denounced. They do not enter into the game of this 'Hegelian-Marxism' that renders sublime the viewpoint of the total historical movement in which ultimately everything finds its meaning. This totalising drift is linked to Marxism itself *as a historical phenomenon.* 'Historical Marxism' is a mixture of 'socialism' and 'communism': this is at least the hypothesis that is set out in the metastructural approach, in the sense that it gives to these terms. It expresses the attractions, born in the time of great industry, between the social forces of power-knowledge (those of competent-elites, above all those of 'competency') and those of the fundamental class. If this account remains pertinent, little wonder that Marxism has an inclination to behave as the party of order, of *a supposed order that is organised among all.* To it, minorities are invisible: they are not part of its historical programme of emancipation. By considering the conditions of the historical social formation of Marxism one can understand its consistency as a political theory: its programme relies on a perspective (structure/tendency) that is inscribed in a horizon of common universality. The apparatuses of sex throw confusion into this historicism. They bring to light 'parts' that are not derivable from the structure of the whole – as the diverse fractions of the fundamental class can be (including the 'excluded') – and whose destiny is not part of the history of this totality, in the great saga of the emancipation of work and its forms of domination. This is what the analysis of sexuality in some sense bears witness to: *there are other histories,* which have their substance, their materiality, their episodes and their own concepts. We can thereby understand that *other combats* have been able, over the decades, to recognise themselves in Foucault's discourse, which is concerned with the liberation of minorities: of prisoners, of homosexuals, of the ill, of the alienated … All these groups have their motives, their forms and their own urgencies, which are derivable not from relations of production (even if they are inseparable from them), but from the diverse management of the body by social power, notably by knowledge-power: management of the sexed body, of the healthy body, of the mortal body. They exist only with their own initiatives and their own discourse. In these conditions, we discern more clearly why 'Marxists', followers of History writ large – and who, despite the polemics, appreciated the epistemologist (notably the Althusserians) – have often shown so little interest in his social critique and in the political conduct that it might suggest.

2. As for the matter of 'race', the question arises in different terms. Here Marx and Foucault criss-cross but without meeting each other. 'Race' is not a concept referring to a real object, since there is no such thing as race: it is a representation (endowed, of course, with real effects) given in a racist relationship. Now, this latter has nothing to do, at least not immediately, with Marx's concepts, namely, those of the class *structure* (and of

state structure at least in the sense that the class structure is in itself statist, superstructural as much as infrastructural). To begin with, the racist relationship participates in a situation that can be defined through the categories of the world-*system*: those of inter-state relations, and more generally of inter-community relations on territories defined on the basis of the plurality inherent in the matrix of the nation state. The space of the world-system, to which 'race' belongs, is only legible through the grammar of the colonialist and imperialist push for capitalist accumulation – an effect of 'structure'. *On the plane of the theoretical configuration,* however, the properly Marxian concepts (those of class *structure*) are in themselves unable to ground a theory of the world-*system*: the (Marxist) theoreticians of the centres–peripheries configuration have in actual fact succeeded in inventing an entirely new grammar unable to be derived from *Capital*.[21] *On the plane of the historical sequence,* Marxism emerged in countries of the Centre as a discourse of the above-defined 'progressist' alliance between 'competent-elites' and the 'working class' – a situation that tended to turn the colony into a subaltern phenomenon, conceived on the basis of the supposedly 'in principle' contradiction between work and capital that was equally part of the field of colonialism. But the difficulties that Marxism encountered in theorising racism stemmed neither from these epistemological

---

[21] And only a metastructural theorisation makes it possible adequately to create the link between both 'dimensions' of the modern form of society, i.e. the (class) structure and the (world-)system – that is at least what I tried to show in *L'Etat-monde*.

conditions, nor from these historical circumstances (which, moreover, did not prevent it from being in the front line in the struggle against colonialism and racism). The fundamental problem lay elsewhere. To understand this discourse of 'race', which supported the domination of the colonisers, another theoretical register to that of Marx and Marxism was required. For the relationship between structure and system intersected here with one of a different nature, namely that between the sexes. In actual fact, at stake here was a *biopolitical* short-circuit between diverse populations and colonial games of power in reproducing them, which is at the same time that of class and system relations, via thousands of conjunctural vicissitudes: appropriation of bodies (servants, wet nurses, mistresses), instrumentalisation of interbreeding, invention of intermediary ethnicities, exultation of differentiated sexual models (western models opposed to others, real or imaginary[22]), etc. All that which, in these processes, pertains to the 'apparatuses of sex', to the articulation of the body and of the population, escapes Marxism and finds expression in the language of Foucault, through the attention he brings to bear on the subjection of bodies, the power-knowledge it exercises and the biopolitical strategies it deploys.[23] Racism has thus to be grasped in this

---

[22] Thus Patricia Hill Collins analyses representations, specific to certain 'whites', of a hyper-developed sexuality among Afro-Americans (see her *Black Feminist Thought*, New York: Routledge, 1990, ch. 6).

[23] See, among others, Ann Stoler's chapter on Foucault in *La Chair de l'Empire: Savoirs intimes et pouvoirs raciaux en regime colonial,* Paris: La Decouverte, 2013. In a similar vein, see Elsa Dorlin, *La Matrice de la race,* Paris: La Decouverte, 2006.

interference between Marx and Foucault, and in the impossible synthesis of their concepts. And one senses the ordeal ahead when one is taken from 'race' to the 'war of races'; as part of a semantics, it is true, that is rather different.

3.3.2 War as an 'analyser of society'

The lectures of 1976, entitled *Society Must Be Defended,* set out from an argument that can be qualified as 'anthropological' insofar as it bears on power, war and peace *in general.* Targeting approaches to *power* in terms of sovereignty or economic domination, Foucault objects that they continue to see power as being about *repression* whereas it in fact pertains to *war.* Power is 'the continuation of war by other means' (*SD*/16). 'War is the very cipher of peace' (*SD*/268). In the beginning is war, not the *logos:* 'the speaking subject is the subject that wages war' (*SD*/54; tm). 'The principle of history' concerns brutality, vigour, contingency, passion, bodies, and chance.[24] These generalities are underlined through a historical investigation in which it is shown that the 'historical consciousness' specific to a 'modern' type of society emerges in a discourse of social 'war' (*SD*/75). It is in terms of war, and more precisely of the 'war of races', that the social classes first become aware of themselves and of their struggles. In confrontation with the

---

[24] The idea is touched upon in diverse passages. He writes, 'The historicity that carries us and determines us is *bellicose*; it is not linguistic. It is a relation of power, not a relation of meaning. History does not have a meaning [...].' It is 'intelligible', analysable, 'but in accordance with the intellibility of struggles, strategies and tactics' (*PK*/114; tm).

discourse of sovereignty and with the then-emergent theories of the contract, this discourse grasps society on the basis not of its possible unity under an order of law, but of its divisions into antagonistic camps, which an insatiable war pits against each other. This paradigm, stemming from the classical age, was common to diverse classes and conflicting powers, which inflected it in various ways. Some highlighted the mythical ancestral rights that invaders had trampled upon and declared one's rights against them – which amounted to a declaration of war against the law in force until the final victory was won. This historical meaning emerged in processes leading from the Middle Ages to modern times. The Levellers and the Diggers are major witnesses of this. With them society ceases to be perceived as a hierarchical body. It is cut in two: rich and poor, masters and dependants.[25] Succeeding the founding pretentions of sovereignty, then, comes the prophecy of emancipation, of a 'revolution' to come. Such is the matrix of this unprecedented and properly modern historical discourse, which is an instrument of struggle, of knowledge and of power. Marx and Engels, via the French historians, discovered in it their basic subject matter.

But, Foucault adds, Marxism ultimately neutralises this paradigm by performing a *dialectical* operation on it: at the end of the revolutionary process, after the final reversal of

---

[25] Luc Foisneau shows how the Foucauldian critique of Hobbes aims at revalorising this English historicism centred on social conflictuality. See 'Hobbes et la critique anti-juridique des Lumieres', in *Lumieres,* No. 8, special issue *Foucault et les Lumieres,* pp. 31–50.

economic domination, antagonism comes to be re-absorbed within a new contractual order of joint concertation among all. But Foucault refuses this final utopia. Under the new forms of state domination, he discerns the war that is begun ever anew. War is indeed the veritable 'analyser of society'. 'The dialectic is the pacification, via the philosophical order, and perhaps via the political order, of this bitter and partisan discourse of basic warfare' (SD/59; tm). Foucault no longer speaks to us here *of a 'truth' pertaining to an era* (in the sense that what *succeeded* the truth of the administrative state was liberal governmentality), but instead of 'truths' that confront each other unilaterally: about 'force relations' that are 'relations of truth' (SD/53). 'The force relation delivers the truth', which is 'a weapon in the force relation' (ibid.). Here, claims to truth asserted by adverse parties are in fact oriented towards the knowledge that might be able to found them. This is how the historical sciences are born, sciences that serve to make war, similar to the other social sciences, whose knowledge is power, and power is war.

But, concerning 'truths', Foucault also proceeds, rather surreptitiously, to perform an entirely different sort of operation: he relates to us the passage from *one truth to another*: from that of race war to that of class struggle. He thus lays down a 'history of truth'. And at the end of this history, he himself enters the stage. He deploys his own knowledge, he delivers us his own 'truth': he indicates what he thinks is the *real* story. What 'class struggle' forgets, he says, is an essential truth that was basic to the 'war of races'. This truth is not of course race, but the war that is declared in its name. The Marxists' dialectic occults the fact of war.

Foucault is indeed not wrong to show that the historical *dialectic* tends toward an end at which the contradiction would have been overcome, toward the social *contract,* which expresses this ambition in advance. This, moreover, is the more pertinent opposition and not so much the one, which he also mentions, between a conservative 'monist' paradigm of *sovereignty* and a *'binary'* revolutionary paradigm of races or classes. For the 'social contract' is available inconsistently depending on whether one is situated above or below – this is a corollary of class confrontation. And, rather than take pleasure in this difference (monist/binary) of kinds of knowledge, he might have instead looked into the question of knowing why both discourses, that of the contract and that of class struggle, emerge *together* within these societies. If this is indeed so, the reason for it is, it seems to me, that far from being foreign to one another they pertain to the same historico-ontological meta/structuration: the former figures the posited presupposition of the latter – the contractual matrix is the posited presupposition of the modern class relationship. This is how Marx undertakes to show that the state structure of class posits the juridico-political metastructure that is its presupposition. This presupposition of (contractual) peace is what 'war', by contrast, cannot offer us: it cannot 'posit' the contract. Nor does it supply the concept of its instrumentalisation. It is therefore inexact to say that 'war is the cipher of peace'. Foucault's discourse, at least at this moment of theoretical provocation,[26] tends inopportunely to combine 'struggle' and 'war' in an indistinct notion of 'battle', making *war* the 'cipher' of social *struggle*. This latter, even in its most peaceable forms, is in many aspects violent, especially when it issues from the top down, since there one possess more ample means of violence – market, organisational, cultural and political. In the chain of its consequences, it is often murderous. But it differs from war, of which murder is the immediate tool, the declared norm. Foucault's wink to Carl Schmitt, for whom the fundamental category is also that of war, of friend/enemy, seems to me to stem from a common lack. Schmitt relativises class struggle by privileging war. Foucault valorises it by qualifying it as war. In each of the discourses, war serves to do damage to struggle. We know that in actual fact both relations combine and cross over with one another. But the (modern class) 'struggle' merits being considered for itself: it differs from 'war' insofar as it refers to a possible general will, as to a 'truth' to which both sides lay claim – in the same terms, in the amphibology of the class relationship – and in this it possesses

---

[26] A concrete analysis obviously produces a more nuanced picture. See the 'Maoist' interview that he gives after his visit to Attica in April 1972. As he says, 'When labour unionisation was founded in order to become recognised it had to distinguish itself from all the seditious groups and all those who refused the juridical order' (*FL*/120; tm). Foucault recognises that this 'quite often served their struggle'. Of course he has in mind a 'struggle' in which he calls, moreover, to associate with other 'truly revolutionary forces' – 'at least that is the opinion of our group', he adds – 'women, prostitutes, homosexuals, drug addicts, there is here a questioning force of society that one has no right, I think, to neglect in the political struggle' (ibid.). It remains that his schema of war as the key to struggle obscures his *theory* of 'political struggle'.

its specific effectiveness. It is only under these conditions that one can grasp the perverse relations between war and struggle, and more generally between relations of right and relations of force.[27]

Once more, then, we are led to place Marx and Foucault not back to back, but face to face, in confrontation with one another. To the axiom 'the history of humanity is the history of class struggle',[28] Foucault opposes, at least at this moment of his research, the following one: 'the motor of institutions and of order is war'.[29] War engenders peace; and it lives on through it. Granted. But we must also *think peace* – the peace

---

[27] Several chapters of *L'État-monde* are devoted to grounding these arguments. I do so, on the one hand, against Carl Schmitt: why are there two 'primary' concepts, in the sense he gives to this term, and not a single one? (see pp. 92–105). On the other, I do so in relation to the perverse interference between war within the world-system and the (class) struggle within the 'world-state' (pp. 268–85).

[28] In *L'État-monde* I tried to show why the Marxian matrix of the mode of production, grasped from within the edifice of the base/superstructure, makes it impossible to conceive war adequately: it is a strictly a-geographical figure. It is the abstract concept of a definite type of social configuration; it says nothing about the *territories* that it configures. It can say nothing about the world system or of war (which is what justifies the Schmittian critique against it). What remains to be done is to produce as rigorous a thinking of the relation of communities to territories as has been done of the relation of classes to the means of production. This is one of the aims of the present work.

[29] 'War obviously presided over the birth of states: right, peace and law were born in the blood and mud of battles. [...] This does not mean, however, that society, law and state are like armistices that put an end to wars, or that they are the products of definitive victories. Law is not pacification, because beneath the law, war continues to rage in all the mechanisms of power, even in the most regular. War is the motor behind institutions and order. In the smallest of its cogs, peace is waging a secret war.' (*SD*/50)

of class or gender struggle – in terms of its specific force, its specific concepts. We must think through its reason – reference point: a *concept* of liberty-equality-rationality – to understand the instrumentalisation of its stakes, its resources and its weaknesses. In war, (claims to) truths are purely antithetical: it's you or us. In struggle, such truths are declared and pitted against one another in the same *conceptual* envelope. But the effects are not the same. Making 'war' into an analyser – elevating it to the commandment – neutralises the operator of 'struggle', the normative presuppositions of which remain in the background in Foucault's work. The moralist certainly continues to be present, but not in the discourse of a moral theory, nor in a positive political theory. He is present in the unsaid, just like negative theology in what it cannot say.[30] And that is the secret of its corrosive power, which remains intact, and is *never compromised*. Imprecation makes heard, more surely than utopian or reformist discourse, the forms of domination inherent in the good order of society. But is this enough if one wants to understand whence comes the force of the people? The power of peace also belongs to it.

3.3.3 'Structure' or 'system'?
Foucault, Habermas and others

The confusion between struggle and war generated by the indistinct discourse of the 'great battle' blurs the difference

---

[30] And as such it remains only a moment of discourse, since nor is it able to think the negative outside of the positive that it produces, outside of its 'productivity'. That is another ambiguous relation that remains for us to think through.

between the types of practice that characterise, respectively, (class) structure and (world-)system. But to understand structure, it must be distinguished from system. The concept of 'structure' advanced in metastructural theory is a *dialectical* one – this term is simply short for the *dialectical relationship* between metastructure, structure and practices. Through it we can conduct a critique of the Habermasian conception of 'system', understood, in accordance with the common sense of liberal tradition, as the articulation between the 'economico-merchant' order and the 'politico-administrative' order.[31] Such a 'system', in a position of exteriority with respect to the 'lived world', appears in some way reified, outside our attainment.[32] If (modern class) *structure* is not to be so understood, namely as a *system* closed on itself, this is because the metastructural presupposition that is posited in modern society is not simply constituted by the duality of both *mediations* market and organisation (which, moreover, by no means correspond to the Habermasian 'systemic' duality, economy *versus* politics), but by the relation, which is given in class struggle, between these *mediations* and the critical discursive *immediacy* that is manifest at their point of antagonistic difference, which is to say, in the amphibological form of their 'difference'. Class *structure* therefore does not constitute a 'system' to which

---

[31] See *L'Etat-monde,* chapters 1 and 2. The figure of the 'metastructural grid', presented above in the Introduction, provides a condensed outline of this point.

[32] Stéphane Haber, for one, directs this critique at him. See *Penser le néocapitalisme,* Paris: Les Prairies ordinaries, 2013. I set out the same sort of argumentation but by taking a metastructural approach.

human actors would be confined: it comprises a continual stake of instrumentalisation and of emancipation. It exists only in its articulation with the *metastructure*: with the 'lived world' of public space, in the broadest sense, in which subjects confront their claims, their 'truths', to say it in Foucauldian fashion. It can 'reproduce' itself only through permanently risking the lived world declared in this inter-discourse, which is inherent to *practices,* the framework of which is defined by modern class structures. This is the weighty sense of the word 'structure', as used in the expression 'class structure': it pertains to the *dialectical relation* between metastructure, structure, and practices.[33]

---

[33] I take the liberty of insisting again that this dialectic is not to be understood as an historical process, in the sense of a dialectics of history, but instead as a *practical process that is always of the instant;* it is filled with intentions and claims (with 'truths') within a framework of structural constraints. In each conjuncture, this practical process grafts a) onto the contingencies of the interrelation between *structural* processes ('relations of production') and technological processes ('productive forces'), and b) through interference with the multiple vicissitudes of their interlinking, onto *systemic* processes (economic, political and cultural processes within the world-*system*), their immediate effects and the long-term perspectives they open. The practical process alone is dialectical; and the concept meta/structure is the one that expresses it. The context of its use is to be related, via theoretical hypotheses and empirical investigations, to particular causes. This is the sense in which Foucault revives the 'event' as part of his opposition to the various structuralisms (*PK*/114). Thinking in terms of the event (*événementaliser*) implies dealing with the multiplicity of causes; it implies 'analysing the event in accordance with the multiple processes that constitute it': those behind the emergence of the prison, those that enable us to decipher the new pedagogy, the professional army, English empirical philosophy, the new division of labour (*DE4*/23–6). The event is always to be *interpreted,* as an arrangement of practical processes, concerning the truths that vie against one another in it. And it is to be

Concerning 'system', we find in contemporary theories of 'global history' a precise use of the term that is in keeping with the concept of 'world-system'. This is the sense in which I have proposed to understand, as a guiding thread for a theory of modernity, the relation between *class structure* (context: the nation state) and the *world-system* (context: between-nations). That formed the point of departure for the reconstruction developed in my *L'Etat-monde* [*World-State*]. Present-day Marxist discourse speaks readily of 'anti-systemic movements', of 'systemic' domination, etc.[34] But this indeterminate use of the term 'system' as regards 'structural' phenomena (similarly to making 'war' the analyser of society) works to eclipse the stakes of the relation between class *structure* and world-*system*, qua two 'dimensions' of the modern form of society.[35] If every event or modern institution can be understood only with this

---

clarified relative to the multiple causalities that meet in it. However, in each case it is only discernible as such relative to the continuities and structural evolutions with which it breaks, and whose nature the historian sets out to determine.

[34] I leave aside the recent lexical reversal performed by the extreme Right insofar as it qualifies itself as 'anti-systemic', stealing a march on an escheated Left. A political analysis of this semantic shift would exceed the limits of this work.

[35] We also see appear here the distinction between the continuum of ideology-utopia, proper to the structure, and racist cryptology, proper to the system; that is, between the amphibological discourse of peace and that of war. Foucault reproaches Hobbes for excluding war from the social body of the republic and turning it purposely into an analyser of the *order between nations*. But Hobbes is not mistaken, only he has no theoretical weapons to understand the social struggle that forms one with the republic, nor therefore its permanent contamination by war within the world-system.

articulation of the structural and the systemic thus understood – for example, between the national and the colonial, between class and 'race', between struggle and war – nothing can be analysed without previously grasping each of these two conceptual orders in themselves, each of which pertains to a specific 'social being'. There must correspond to this a definite terminological distinction enabling us to express the interrelations. The discourse of racism is one of a world-system at war (centres/peripheries, on a small or large scale, from the global to the local), of a sexuated system in which populations confront each other as class-inflected nation states.

It should be recognised that it is Foucault, more than any other master thinker, who has impacted on reflections and research undertaken on the acronym class/sex/race, and notably also on those who, in addition, refer to Marxism. The renewal he effects is tied to the centrality that the sort of materialist nominalism to which he incessantly returns us attributes to the *body*. The body is at once always a class body (and inflected through a class state), a sexed body and a racial body (pertaining to the system). Feminist as well as colonial and postcolonial studies have all had reason to identify with this. Slavery, interbreeding, migrations, imprisonment, sexing, subalternities, racisms, discriminations, resistances – on such issues Foucault is omnipresent, providing us with an inexhaustible source of inspiration. The 'Marxists', too, ought to learn to recognise this as their good, *as a common good originating elsewhere.* What they can thus *admit* from Foucault falls under two distinct rubrics. On the one hand, as we saw in the preceding chapter, Foucault identifies, in the terms of knowledge-power, *the other pole* of the dominant class, which operates parallel to property-power. On the other hand, and even if, as some feminists have reproached him, he does not tackle gender relations, he contributes, notably through what he teaches us about this power-knowledge, to an identification – alongside the social relationship of class (and of system) – of the *other primary social relation,* the social relation of sex, of sexual reproduction, which is endowed with another historicity, another political temporality, one of which every 'minority' also partakes. From there we get the criss-crossed relations between the structure of class, world-system and sexed relations, relations through which 'race' is defined qua ideological fact and social configuration.

Marx and Foucault have been presented here as analysts of overarching processes and individual singularities. One accomplishes this in terms of 'structure', the other in terms of 'apparatuses'. And in each of these figures, both holism and nominalism – the macro and the micro – interpenetrate and support one another. Depending on the particular case, however, philosophical priority seems to be given either to holism or to nominalism, to the extent that two distinct research fields are triggered and incomparable effects of knowledge are determined. Hence, the temptation arises to identify Marx as the thinker of the totality and Foucault as the thinker of the subject, at the risk of splitting them from one another and banalising them both. The terms of cooperation between both approaches thus seem to present themselves not as an attempt to surpass the *philosophical* tension, which would rather lead to neutralising both approaches, but – and this is what I have attempted to show – as one of *theoretical* reconstruction, the aim being to develop a theory of the modern form of society. To test the solidity of this reconstruction it is essential to examine the relation it enables us to establish between the two main bodies of concepts used respectively by Marx and Foucault in the analysis of modern society: 'capitalism' and 'liberalism'.

4

MARX'S 'CAPITALISM' AND FOUCAULT'S 'LIBERALISM'

Marx and Marxists after him characterise the social order that thrived after the second half of the eighteenth century as 'capitalism' and make out a future they call socialism (or communism). In the first instance, Foucault explicitly claims his belonging to this tradition, or at least his adherence to the reference to capitalist class domination as that which is to be abolished. Yet by end of the 1970s we see him arrive at an examination of the modern social order in terms of 'liberalism'. In so doing, he discerns beyond the horizon of the decades-long existence of the social-state the premises of a neoliberalism to come. The diagnostics and prognostics he formulates are clearly to be interpreted in accordance with the content and status of the two concepts that this discernment foregrounds – namely 'capitalism' and 'liberalism' – one of which announces the search for profit and the other, a politics of life, a 'biopolitics'.

In Foucault's lectures of 1978 and 1979, the concept of 'biopolitics' comes to constitute the kernel of an investigation that takes as its object a set of economico-political institutions and practices that no longer concerns individuals (such as in his research of 1972–74 on 'political anatomy' in which he treats the ill, students, the mad, prisoners, soldiers and so on), but instead *populations* in their entirety and the maximisation of the life of the social body as such. This term 'biopolitics' contains two successive meanings. First, it refers to the emergence of a 'police' in the old sense of the word, one associated with mercantilism and entailing state initiative in all domains. The remainder of Foucault's account then deals with the period that begins in 1850 and takes biopolitics, on the contrary, as the proper of 'liberalism' in the modern sense of *state minimisation*.

In the Marxist perspective, as we know, things proceed wholly differently: the economic processes favoured by liberalism generate a *maximisation of the state* as an instance of class power. At the same time, however, Marx credits the capitalist system with a specific civilisational productivity, which leads it – with time – to be overcome as an effect of the capacities it unleashes among the exploited themselves and the potentialities it disseminates throughout society as a whole.

In other terms, Marx has in his sights the dynamics of capitalism and Foucault (in the years 1977–79) has in his the rationality of liberalism. That is to say, we have two approaches here that pertain to different theoretical ambitions. The former deciphers a *structure of society*: capitalism refers to a certain 'mode of production', and entails a superstructure with which it becomes one. The latter, of course, maintains a reference to capitalism as an economic system, but its proper object is liberalism as a *practice of government*. Marx sought to produce a *general code* that would enable us to decipher the entire set of social processes, for the purpose of envisaging an alternative strategy: he studies practices (capitalist, worker) insofar as they partake of structures and the historical tendencies of these structures. Foucault, who objects to any project of theoretical or practical totalisation, presents only *points of view* – on the basis of concepts such as those of discipline, norm, biopolitics, power-knowledge, liberalism – opening up perspectives on this ensemble. It remains that his diverse concepts, which all work to shed light on one another, together form a sort of constellation and permit designations – disciplinary society, society of control, medicalised society – that are presented in superimposition rather than in succession, thus forming a certain image of modern society. And what he thus discovers in the modern past, sedimented in successive layers, appears strikingly actual. His conceptuality, in this comparable to Marxism, thus generates a certain 'vision of the world' in which we live. More precisely: a certain idea of what is produced in it, of the conditions in which it produces something. In sum, Marx and Foucault present us, one under the paradigm of capitalism, the other under that of liberalism, with certain outlooks concerning the production of humans (of 'subjects') and of society in the conditions of modernity.

It is on the basis of this schema – which is that of a 'social productivity' specific to our time – that I propose to compare their respective approaches and to articulate them together beyond their contradictions. The question is ultimately to assess the value of these labels – capitalism, liberalism, neoliberalism – for an understanding of the modern and contemporary world and its becoming. Are they instruments of knowledge or epistemological obstacles? What can we expect from these concepts, from their performance on the battlefield of the social sciences and political philosophy?

To judge this, we must return to the *biopolitical* essence of Marx's analysis, in which is elaborated the principle of movement and the contradictions of 'capital', and which generates a conceptual constellation in which liberalism can be deconstructed. I again argue, however, that this approach is incomplete, insofar as it prevents an understanding of the entirety of the process of production specific to modern society, thus leaving in the shadows the other 'pole', that of 'knowledge-power', which is economic as much as political (§4.1). Foucault takes this latter pole as the privileged object of his critical investigation, following a paradoxical line that ultimately returns him to the Marxian terrain of 'capital', positioning him as a narrator of a new kind. In what follows, I take up his path through the prison and the courts, the hospital and the asylum – all the way to 'government' (§4.2).

4.1 THE HISTORICAL PRODUCTIVITY OF CAPITALISM

Foucault was disinclined to discourse about the contradiction between 'capital and labour'. He preferred to speak in terms of 'antagonism', of a mutual *agonism*. Power is a confrontation, in which resistance sort of continuously 'recharges' it, and vice versa. Weighing on the concept of contradiction, however, is a tare, namely the facility with which it often becomes the operator of its own overcoming. The 'development of the contradictions of capitalism' announces its ineluctable end. This end nevertheless seems, just like the horizon, to keep receding as one approaches it … Foucault is therefore right to proceed in his thinking counter to this teleological mode. In my view, however, this does not mean that every schema of 'contradiction' can be dismissed. I suggest taking Marx's analysis further by articulating two concepts that I designate, respectively, as the 'political contradiction' (§4.1.1) and the 'productive contradiction' (§4.1.2) of capitalism. What I call *Marx's biopolitics* receives expression in the relation between these terms, and it cannot fail to enter into conflict with Foucault's own biopolitics. This elaboration of questions, ones that remain implicit in standard Marxism, must in my view enable a confrontation with Foucault over the question of knowing what sort of 'productivity' can be specifically attributed to modern society.

4.1.1 The political contradiction of capitalism

Capitalism's most general contradiction is not a simple economic contradiction between capital and work, one which would flow from the fact that the exploitation of wage labour defines opposed interests and requires, at the same time as ensures, a relation of domination, faced with which workers are prompted to resist, to the point of taking up the goal of overturning it. I distance myself from this guiding schema of *Capital,* insofar as it suggests that the proletariat, concentrated in large-scale industry, will end up coming to appropriate the means of production and to open a new era founded on the abolition of the market, itself to be replaced with democratic planning. The metastructural approach, according to which in the modern form of society the dominant class contains two poles, moves us away from such outlooks. And yet it continues, as we shall see, to be nourished by Marx's conceptual elaboration.

The Marxian analysis is in actual fact far subtler. It puts forward an analysis of the wage relation which, *in linking it to the market,* shows that the latter implies the wage earner's official recognition as a free person, contractually able to dispose of himself and, in this sense at least, equal – in a relation of wage exploitation founded on a market relation. This freedom, beyond the free use of the wage, points to the ability to change bosses. Commentators tend all too often to reduce this freedom to this ability, namely to the possibility to be exploited by another. And as such that this freedom is illusory. But this is not the case. For this ability to change one's master, insofar as it exists practically, confers on the worker a certain power over the latter, a small power that from the beginning requests only obscure sites, but decisive sites for those concerned, in which he will be able to invest this power – those places of the 'detail' to which Foucault attached so much importance. A potential power thus attaches to the metastructural conditions of the wage labourer, that is to say, to the *declared* freedom that formed a constant structural provocation in the confrontation with patronal power. A principle of agonism, one dear to Foucault: power is a reciprocal relation. And all the more so as the declared contractual freedom of the wage labourer is *formally* indissociable from the freedom to contract with others (workers) for the purpose of organisation – indissociable at least in the discourse of equality among all, a posited presupposition of the modern form of class society. And psychologists of work show us how this process can emerge whenever several persons are summoned to cooperate in a single undertaking: they find themselves incited to make known a common freedom.

In truth, the logic of capitalism contains a tendency to slavery, and this pertains to both *dimensions of the modern form of society* – system and structure.[1] Corresponding to the capitalist wage system of the centres is the capitalist slavery of the peripheries. But, as we know, this threat now exists in the centre itself. From the *'systemic'* side – as the Arendtian account shows, according to which 'human rights' exist only as 'citizen rights' – the slavery apparatuses of colonial capitalism consisted in the exclusion of the population concerned from the community of the nation state, and *thereby* from the human community, that of human rights. From the *'structural'* side, in the wage system as such, patronal power does not possess the same facility, but it *always* seeks to appropriate for itself the ability to be able to dismiss its wage labourers as it pleases, that

---

[1] This is a central topic of *L'État-monde,* Here I remain within the limits of Marx's thinking, which holds fast to the 'structural' dimension of the clas- sist nation state, as against the 'systemic' dimension of the 'world-system'.

is to say, to render them dependent through precarity. As soon as the circumstances allow, it will proceed in this fashion. In countries of the centre, the increasingly generalised practice of 'internships', as indefinite preconditions for real employment, provides a labour supply that, not acquired permanently, can be disposed of at will and thrown out of employment. Today this works to establish a socialised slavery in the form of wage earners without wages.[2] The secular class struggle that has been waged to date for the legislation of the working day is thus doubled by a struggle around the very concept of the wage system, around the wage institution as such.

The modern recognition of freedom, to the extent that it effectively exists, does not play out in the inter-individuality of the wage earner/employer relation, but in class confrontation *within the nation state,* where producers learn from experience

---

2 An example of this occurred in France with the attempt to implement the CPE (*contrat de premiere embauche*; first employment contract) in 2006, a bill that was postponed thanks to a massive rallying of the population. Situations of dependency on class, race or sex, the sites of which are diverse but often interpreted as simple leftovers of the past, thus have to do with structural-systemic relations of force. [Trans. – In Spring 2006 the then French prime minister Dominique de Villepin introduced the 'first employment contract', a new form of contract for people under twenty-six years of age designed to exempt employers from giving reasons when dismissing employees within an initial two-year 'trial period'. The contract was part of a bill called the Equality of Opportunity Act established on 31 March 2006. As Bidet notes above, the Act was so unpopular that massive protests were staged across France, forcing a government backdown. The part of the Act pertaining to the CPE was repealed on 21 April 2006, thanks to a bill called Youth Access to Professional Life in Firms, but other contested components of the original Act were maintained.]

that civil freedom between-each-person is contentless without the exercise of civic freedom among all (and in reciprocal fashion) in the key fields of work and life – around which the class relationship of force is constituted. *Capitalism's most general contradiction* therefore consists not only in an opposition of interests between exploiters and exploited. It is not flatly economic. It is also political in nature. It resides in the fact that modern exploitation consists in the domination of workers designated as free and from then on led to get organised and to rebel – and to lay claim to a power of state. It is a contradiction in terms. It is a *real* contradiction, one played out in the circle of metastructure/structure/practices. In the class nation-state, capitalist domination cannot ever exist without the risk of a constant threat: that pertaining to the declared freedom of the wage-earning citizen, which contains the potential for concerted action between wage-earning citizens and others beholden to capital.

This political contradiction is *biopolitical* in nature. A Marxian biopolitics certainly exists.[3] It can be understood on the basis of the primary concept of value as 'expenditure of labour power', that is to say 'productive expenditure of the brain, muscles, nerves and hands of men'. The capitalist interface of that expenditure, Marx explains, is the 'consumption' of wage

---

[3] 'The biopolitical body of *Capital*', to which the following statements refer back, is the topic of the first chapter of *Le Néolibéralisme, Un autre grand récit*, Paris: Les Prairies Ordinaires, 2016. It contains, notably, the various expressions that I have noted here by placing them in inverted commas, but situates and analyses them in their contexts.

labour power by the employer. At stake is precisely the *life* of the worker. And it takes the form of a *political* relation between partners who declare themselves free, in market terms. For, while the capitalist does of course have the worker at work 'at his disposal', this latter retains a 'self-disposal', and can change masters. This is not simply a matter of the commodities to be produced, but of the 'reproduction of labour power', which is key to the confrontation between both partners, that is, to the very life of workers, its quality and duration. Such is in fact the object of the primary, secular confrontation around the 'working day', which governs the worker's longevity. This concept finds its place in the 'economy' of only one theory, namely Marx's. And the place it comes to have is central, as we see in reading the (very long) chapter 10 of Book 1, which carries the title 'The Working Day'. The concepts of the theory of value and surplus value are of a nature as to be both economic-quantitative *and* political, or more precisely biopolitical. The worker is exploited as a free person – to the extent that something of this sort is produced – only because he can, in some fashion, assert that freedom as presuming the ability to associate with others in a class struggle that enables it to be shored up. This association, Marx shows, culminates in the 'legislation of the working day', that is in the creation of a law not in thrall to the market. This logic of life arises counter to capitalist logic, which is that of capitalists as such, each of whom has as his end the accumulation of abstract wealth, surplus value, which is the only means by which he can continue to subsist in the competition against his rivals. It is at this moment only, upon the assertion of a *citizen* right to work, that the (economico-political) theory of surplus value, of the capitalist management of value, is *conceptually* completed. But, as we see, it is accomplished only at the point of its surpassing, when it appears that market right, as soon as it is affirmed as freedom, encounters the polar opposition between a claim to a freely organised order among all and the logic of surplus value. This is not a dialectic of history but instead of the event, of daily struggle, which is crystallised in advances and retreats.

4.1.2 The productive contradiction of capitalism

I designate as 'productive contradiction' the one that is presented, correlatively to the 'political contradiction', in accordance with the other, economic 'face' of the capitalist structure. Here the entire biopolitical programme inherent in the problematic that Marx opened is revealed. Several epistemological obstacles nonetheless clutter our path. The first pertains to the traditionally proposed interpretation of this contradiction by philosopher-commentators. The second flows from the specifically limited character that Marx gives to his analysis of the economy. And the third comes from the extensive use generally made of the term 'capitalism'.

1. *The 'contradiction of capital' is established not between use-value and value, as is generally said in philosophical glosses, but between use-value and surplus-value.*

Let's take up the distinction that Marx makes in Book 1, chapter 7 of *Capital* between 'production in general', which is the production of *use-values*, and 'properly capitalist production', which is the production of *surplus-value*. Productive contradiction resides in the fact that capitalists cannot reap surplus value without having commodities, and thus use-values, produced. Clearly, when it comes to financial capital, there are some who manage to shed this task onto others, but it must nonetheless be ultimately guaranteed: to produce commodities, that is to say, *use-values*, which are lived as such insofar as they find takers on the market. But – and here is where the *contradiction* is introduced into the *production* process – which use-values are to be produced and for which consumers? Private jets or trams? Prisons or public schools? Palatial clinics or hospitals open to all? This is precisely the concrete stake of the capital/*labour* contradiction. But this latter is part of a larger contradiction between capitalists and the *population in general*. The issue is evidently one of the 'population', of its individual and collective life: which is to say, in Foucault's language, of 'biopolitics'. For, if the logic of capitalists is profit, it tends to establish itself (through its commercial, political and cultural hold) irrespectively of its consequences *for populations* and their cultures, and for nature. In this, productive contradiction is a contradiction between the *logic of surplus-value* and the *logic of use-values,* which is observable in the everyday confrontation between people – that is, workers and citizens – and the capitalist class. It bears on the choice of which use-values to produce and on the *conditions* of their production, which are in themselves collective use-values, and which govern the 'production' of individuals themselves. This choice is determined by the wage and fiscal, ideological, and political relation of force, bound notably to the relative hold of the private or public sectors over the means of production.

'Productive contradiction', we see, is articulated together with 'political contradiction'. Marx's account tackles the capitalist class relation as an apparatus in which the worker, supposedly recognised as free and equal and rational, finds himself impelled to respond to the power accumulated via surplus value by engaging in concerted resistance against universal *commodification,* by intervening in the *organisation* of society, and thus by manifesting a capacity to decree the production of determinate use-values in determinate conditions. This comprises the crucible of the modern class struggle, on the basis of which struggles for socialism and communism are to be grasped. The terrain is precisely that of a *class biopolitics,* which exists as such only by asserting itself in the state sphere. The 'population', far from being the simple preoccupation of government, comes to be concerned with itself and its own 'government'.[4]

In short, it pays to understand that this 'productive contradiction' bears on the relation between use-value *and surplus-value.* So by no means does it concern a 'contradiction between use-value *and value*'. This theoretical confusion, common in

---

[4] On this topic, *pace* Foucault, who attaches little importance to the popular rebellions on which the theories he analyses are formulated, see Déborah Cohen, 'La population contre le peuple', *Labyrinthe* No. 22, Paris, 2005, pp. 67–79. She writes: 'Although put through the riddle of a knowledge-power that objectivises it, which will tend to turn subjects bearing wills into objects to be controlled, the population nevertheless remains the people.'

the standard exegesis of philosophers, leads one to impute all of capitalism's pathology to the market. It forbids us from grasping the fact that anticapitalist combats for emancipation have every reason to orient themselves not towards the abolition of the market, but towards control of the market via organisation (socialism) and control of the organisation via radical democracy (communism). Such is in fact the daily bread of class struggle, and it is the only revolutionary horizon it can be given.

2. *What nevertheless prevents Marxism from experimenting in all its scope with this logic of social emancipation is the incompleteness of the Marxian analysis of work in modern society, which is to be read on two distinct registers.*

On the side of modern organised production: the approach taken in *Capital* allows this articulation between political contradiction and economic contradiction to appear. But it neglects the fact that 'organisation *is in itself* (and not by the sole fact of appearing in the capitalist firm) a class factor, and that it also contains, in the manner of the market, its own potential for productive irrationality. The experience of 'real socialism', in which organisation was substituted for the market, revealed as though under a magnifying glass a potential that has been borne out, to diverse degrees, in all versions of modern society. The meagre attention that Marxists have paid to this phenomenon has to have reasons that can be located in its history: *Marxism* expresses at once the rationality and the ambivalence of the historical relation of alliance between competent-elites (still in the sense of those who 'have' competency) and the *fundamental class;* and this is why it oscillates between socialism and communism. Organisational domination as such remains outside of the *theoretical* field of Marxian critique, even if it intervenes in its *descriptive* register.

On the side of non-capitalist modern production: the 'critique of the political economy' that Marx advanced suffers from an overly narrow view of economic space. It is indeed crucial to have a solid grasp of the *limits* of the object of study fixed by the designation 'mode of capitalist production'. The rigour of Marxian analysis – and what makes it suited to research in the field of the capitalist economy – has as its flipside that diverse sections of social production remain in the shadows, stricken from the agenda. The model of the 'mode of capitalist production' rigorously circumscribes the field of capitalist production: its ultimate object is profit and its ultimate constraint is the production of commodities, as this enables the accumulation of capital in the hands of owners of means of production and exchange. This model thus defines its own limits, which Marxist culture understands only laterally. *Capital* thus begins with that highly problematic sentence: 'The wealth of societies in which the capitalist mode of production prevails appears as an immense collection of commodities.' This statement can be justified: Marx's object of focus is not *production in general* in this type of society, but instead only *capitalist* production, which is a production *of commodities* (or services) with a view to making a profit. But he surreptitiously conceals a part of the problem he evokes. In effect, 'by wealth', as he stresses, he does not mean value, but instead 'use-value'.

If this is so, he should have counted in the wealth produced in 'societies in which the mode of capitalist production reigns' not only commodities, but also the product of work created for the purpose of familial self-consumption in the form of *care* services, the work product of functionaries of all orders and that of every kind of self-employed worker. He deploys another logic here than that of the (capitalist) *market*: beyond a mode of purely personal or associative cooperation (or dedication), it is a matter of diverse modes of *organisation* of the labour force in accordance with overall plans and hierarchies of competency. Marx identified this *organised* mode as the one that presides over the 'division of labour' *within the firm,* in contrast with the market division (i.e. coordination) of labour between firms. And he put these two pairs of 'division of labour' at the centre of his study on the dynamics of capitalism. But his investigation is limited to the context of the capitalist enterprise, to the circle of production for profit.[5] It ought to have led him to analyse the

---

5 Marx's account, which is based on a theory of value defined in the market relation, stumbles on the consideration of non-market production in modern societies. This is the other, economic part of the questions under examination here. All treatment of it in terms of the 'non-productive labour' required for the reproduction of labour power lacks any sociological realism. Attaching to this are the diverse problems that today fuel discussions around the calculation of GDP, but this exceeds the scope of the present study. They concern all theories of 'capitalism' or of 'socialism'. See my debate with Jean-Marie Harribey on MATIS (http://perso.orange.fr/jacques.bidet). Harribey reformulates his replies to my questions in *La Richesse, la Valeur et l'Inestimable* Paris: LLL, 2013, pp. 370–5. My 2003 presentation has also been published under the title 'Objections addressées a Jean-Marie Harribey', in *ContreTemps,* No. 20, Paris: Syllepse, 2014, pp. 119–25.

'organisational division' of work as a transversal form within modern society taken in its entirety.

Foucault would come to orient himself around precisely this other form of social space. And this would occur not along the lines of a division of territory that might enable a peaceable division of theoretical tasks, but along the lines of a muted conceptual *disagreement* over the concept of 'production', the trigger for which was the scheme of 'knowledge-power'. This epistemic crisis can be resolved only through an overcoming carried out through a completely different representation of the modern social structure: that suggested in the metastructural approach. But this compels us to reconsider the very concept of capitalism and the use able to be made of it.

3. *What is 'capitalism?' An epistemological obstacle.*

It will not have escaped the reader that I give to 'capitalism' a sense that is hardly in keeping with the most common use of this term. This is not a simple question of terminology. I contest the very notion that Marxists, and many others besides, usually entertain of 'capitalism', and notably in current debates on its resurgence, its infinite resilience or its proclaimed end. What I challenge is that fact of designating as 'capitalism' the set of what is produced in so-called capitalist societies, in societies where, as Marx says, 'the mode of capitalist production reigns'. My critique is addressed, among others, to currents such as the Wertkritik, or New Critique of Value, illustrated by authors such as Robert Kurtz and Moishe Postone, for whom capitalist accumulation is that of abstract work or of dead work. This representation of capitalism in terms of fetishism and abstraction is certainly of such a nature as to feed the critical discourses that develop around universal commodification and financialisation. But it does not make it possible to comprehend, in these processes of globalisation, the effective or potential part of the fundamental or popular class, nor that of 'power-knowledge'; nor does it allow us therefore to conceive of some strategy of emancipation. The concept of 'productive contradiction of capitalism' is the one that enables us to think these diverse terms *together.* If the modern state is preoccupied with life, this is because, it seems to me, it is not entirely in the hands of a 'capitalist class'. This can also be seen in reverse: to the extent that, in the neoliberal process, the capitalist pole of the dominant class dominates in a more exclusive fashion, hegemonising that of 'competency', life is effectively placed in greater danger – that of humans and numerous other species. But the marvels of our collective life are not the fact of capital. The term 'capitalism' is an epistemological obstacle as soon as it is taken for the concept, or the key, of the modern social whole. Some consequences flow from this for the analysis of liberalism and neoliberalism.[6]

---

6 The topic advanced by Stéphane Haber of 'reflective capitalism', of the biopolitical productiveness proper to neocapitalism, seeks to avoid these peculiarities. See 'Du néolibéralisme au néocapitalisme? Quelques réflexions à partir de Foucault', in his *Actuel Marx,* No. 51, *Néolibéralisme: Rebond/Rechute,* Paris: PUF, 2012, pp. 59–72, and *Penser le néocapitalisme. Vie, capital et aliénation,* Paris: Les Prairies ordinaires, 2013. In the terms of the preceding metastructural analysis, it is clear that that fecund idea of 'reflexivity' comes to be used not on the basis of an entity designated in its unity, such as 'capitalism', but on the interplay of the three primary 'social forces', which are the focus of a theory of 'regimes of hegemony', to

4.2 THE HISTORY OF 'LIBERALISM'

Despite the possible impression of a quasi-Marxist Foucault in 1971–73 undergoing a slow mutation to becoming a quasi-liberal in 1977–79, we can discern in his approach a deep epistemological continuity, which is notably manifest in the constancy of a definite conception of the 'productivity' of social apparatuses of knowledge-power. He very precisely adopts in his own way the *general concept of production* understood as 'production of utilities' (*alias* use-values), to which the (Marxian) 'critique of the economy' opposes the *specific concept of production* proper to the productive logic of capitalism: the production of 'surplus value'. But paradoxically, he is able to open a larger field of analysis by taking a theoretical backward step in relation to Marx – by blotting out the race to gain 'abstract' wealth – and this is what motivates the metastructural reconstruction of Marxism (§4.2.1). This concept of production will provide a certain coherence to his progression from penal 'discipline' to the apparatuses of sexuality and to liberal politics over the course of the decade (§4.2.2). It leads, however, to a reversal of perspective that neutralises the class relationship within a relation between governors and 'the governed' (§4.2.3). From there a problematic of 'governmentality' emerges that leaves no place for the revolutionary question of self-government (§4.2.4).

---

be presented in my book *Le Néolibéralisme, Un autre grand récit*, Paris: Les Prairies Ordinaires, 2016.

4.2.1 'Discipline' as productive of utility-docility

In its relation to that of power-knowledge, the concept of 'discipline', as presented in *Discipline and Punish,* defines a *general* trait of modern society. Related to the concept of organisation, it enables an enlargement of Marx's analysis of class. It adheres both to the Weberian register of 'rationalisation' and to the Frankfurtian register of 'instrumental reason'. But it contributes to a more precise characterisation insofar as it links knowledge and power, norm and productivity, in conformity with the singular constellation supposed characteristic of a time when the truth of reference resided in science and its accompanying technique.

'Discipline' appears as a new principle of order common to diverse social modern 'apparatuses', whence emerges a new form of individualisation. It implies, as we saw, a colonisation of *space* (closure, surveillance, ranks, places, itineraries …) and of *time* (ordered and full schedules, and a standardisation of the acts, tasks and stages comprising them). It thus enables the *classification* of individuals with regard to the tests of which this spatio-temporal framework furnishes the theatre: hierarchisation, marking, distinction, decreeing of norms, archiving, examination and diverse pathways to excellence or exclusion. It aims at integral social *control*, of which the *panopticon* illustrates the concept. Through its multiple grids, as *knowledge* it reaches the *individual itself*,[7] whose singular

---

[7] Foucault says, 'All the great disciplinary machines, barracks, schools, workshops and prisons, are machines that make it possible to define the individual.' They have individualising effects: 'The individual has become an essential stake of power' (*DE3*/550-1).

characteristics it singles out, as well as its status as normal or abnormal, and its potential utility or dangerousness. As *power* over beings which are thus individualised, it is exercised as a last resort on *bodies*, which it disciplines, corrects, punishes, mobilises for work and for combat, instructs, educates, cures. In short, it is productive insofar as it produces beings that are both *docile* and *productive*. According to a formulation that recurs and insists throughout *Discipline and Punish*, the disciplines become 'general formulas of domination'; they converge in that they 'impose a relation of docility-utility'.[8] I set out to consider this conceptual couple in its difference to the perspective that Marx opens (that of 'productivity' in terms of surplus value as a logic of capital): this is an analytical backward step that proves paradoxically fecund.

Utility

1. The sort of 'utility' – let's start with that – focused on by Foucault concerns, it seems to me, both the effect produced, the capacity of the producer to produce it, and the production of such a producer. The healthy, instructed, well-trained, possibly corrected individual is useful in that it is able to produce socially useful effects. It is, in this sense,

---

[8] 'Docile bodies' (p. 162), which are the focus of the chapter, are endowed with 'capacities' and 'aptitudes' (p. 165). This discipline produces subjected and practised bodies, 'docile bodies'. Disciplines increase the forces of the body (in economic terms of utility) and diminish these same forces (in political terms of obedience) (p. 138). Military and industrial disciplines heighten capacities, aptitudes, as do schools: 'The disciplines function increasingly as techniques for making useful individuals' (p. 211).

'productive'. The logic of forms of knowledge-power would be to work at producing such individuals, or at selecting them. We have noted by which means this occurs. Marx's analysis of the division of labour in manufacturing and the factory (in chapters 14 and 15 of Book 1 of *Capital*), in fact also presents us with an approach of this type. It consists in the invention of a measured space/time that is filled and emptied of all its 'pores', the surveyed and controlled mobilisation of bodies to the rhythm of the machine, a normalisation of acts, a standardisation of criteria, expectations and exigencies, a programmation of activities and interrelations, an hierarchical organisation – and, correlative with this, new 'subjects' that correspond to these conditions. But Foucault, who, we saw, refers to these texts and adopts this model of the factory in a specific way, diverges from it on two points.

On the one hand, he *generalises* it to encompass the set of modern social apparatuses. Put otherwise, the theme of discipline, re-elaborated on the basis of the carceral institution, is outlined as a universal matrix that guarantees communication between diverse kinds of knowledge and the articulation of diverse powers: military, managerial, medical, judiciary, pedagogical ... Carceral power crosses over with the legal power to punish, the disciplinary power of educating, curing and making work, as far as 'the terrorism of the production line' (*DE3*/587). The phenomenon is circular. The edict of the efficient penalty presumes knowledge, discernment, distinctions. Judges, urged to distinguish between the normal and the a-normal, balk at this difficulty and summon specialists on the social nature of individuals: doctors, psychiatrists, educators. They deem a 'man knowable' by human science, laboratories in which, in answering these new demands, the infinite register of *norms* is elaborated. In short, discipline becomes a general concept, in this way qualifying modern society, which is a disciplinary society as much as a market one. But, if this is the case, this is because it participates in power-knowledge, which runs transversally across society.

On the other hand, we see that Foucault *positivises* the model by placing disciplinary power under the aegis of knowledge. In this sense, the institutional apparatuses described are oriented towards efficacy, towards heightening the performance levels of the individuals concerned (*DP*/137). They emerge, or at least come into their full development, at the time of the Enlightenment, in which *public utility* becomes the universal reference in terms of justice, health, administration, etc., fuelling reforms and utopias (e.g. Cesare Beccaria …). This power-knowledge supposedly knows what is useful and is familiar with the means of producing it. It is nevertheless not to be taken as Reason in History. For it is inflected in the plural. If its diverse institutional practices thus produce a new being, it is not as a social power, as a *general intellect,* of which each person would be the expression: it is through an intertwining of distinct and incomparable powers, which, participating in the same social logic, that of *power-knowledge*, nevertheless go towards achieving an overarching result.

Brought thus to light in its generality and its positivity, this is the *structural* 'continent' (in the sense of the structure of class) that Foucault discovered. It is incumbent on us, however, to push him further. Foucault sets out from an analysis of *practices* before moving back up to the material and discursive institutional *apparatuses* in which they are exercised. It remains for us then to move from the apparatus to the *structure* into which it is inserted. And in order to do this – at least this is what I've tried to show (§3.1.2) – we must consider the inter-individual 'mediations' constitutive of this structure: market and organisation. We thus understand – this is the interpretation I am putting forward – that what Foucault effectively 'discovered' is an order that, by contrast with that of the *market* (and as its '*other* pole'), unfolds not as an a posteriori equilibrium among the initiatives of producers in competition with one another, but as an a priori *organisation* of means with a view to achieving ends, variously defined by particular kinds of knowledge. But this order – and here is the decisive point – is not elaborated from on high, from the summit of the state machinery: instead, it emerges from below, from 'civil society', that is to say, it emerges in an immediately fragmented form, in the framework of the diverse 'vital' functions – school, enterprise, hospital, prison ... – entailed in the complexity of modern society. These comprise simply so many sites of power-knowledge in confrontation and competition. If these sorts of knowledge-power can nevertheless cooperate this is because *together* they compose *another* power – one that has its own logic, that of a form of knowledge made up of interconnected kinds of knowledge – that associates and clashes in contradictory fashion with the power of the proprietor in the modern class relationship, and is regularly mixed in with it in the guise of grand 'strategies'. If such is the case, it is possible, it seems to me, to move from Foucault-type *practices* to Marx-type *structures*. But this presumes that we enlarge the Marxian structural schema: the dominant class contains two poles, namely property-power *and* knowledge-power. These are the constituents of a realist tableau of the modern class relationship.

2. It seems remarkable to me, at once logical and para-doxical, that Foucault makes this discovery by turning away from the point on which Marx focuses: the capitalist class relationship understood as a relation of *exploitation*, in the analytico-theoretical sense of a production of surplus-value. Foucault takes up chapter 15 of Book 1, 'Machinery and Large-Scale Industry', but he ignores chapter 7, 'The Labour Process and the Valorisation Process', the object of which is precisely to show that in capitalism the verb 'to produce' is to be taken in *these two distinct senses* (i.e. to produce use-values and to produce surplus-value). It is, as is well known, through this distinction that Marx establishes his theory of 'exploitation'.[9] That is the pivotal point of the entire construction of *Capital*. The work process *in general* is oriented toward the production of a *utility*, or more precisely of 'use-values'. The properly *capitalist* work process, or valorisation process, possesses, in

---

[9] The English rendering of the title is close to the original German version *Arbeitprozeß und Verwertungsprozeß*. While the French rendering, *Proces de travail et proces de valorisation*, which was most certainly dictated by Marx, differs, it does have the merit of indicating more directly the problem concerning us here.

addition, its own specific logic, in that its ultimate aim is *surplus-value,* or profit, which can only ensue from the fact that the waged worker produces a value that is greater than his salary. Some will say that everyone *knows,* and not least of all Foucault, that wage-earners produce profit by producing useful things (commodities), and that this is the objective of the capitalists that employ them. *But this does not constitute a theory.* Marx undertook to theorise this contradictory relation between the concreteness of utility and the abstraction of profit; and in arriving at that point he had to proceed to the prior construction of a theory of value (called 'theory of labour-value', and let's note that on this basis he will come, at the end of his analysis, to the historical process of capitalist accumulation at the global scale). Foucault, by contrast, aims at the *general* fact of a knowledge-power (in its modern form), in some domain, 'economic' or otherwise, of its exercise. He therefore remains at a *general* notion of production as the production of 'utility'. This doing, he turns away from Marx's theorisation and its most decisive aspect for an understanding and critique of modern society. He remains at the context that *Capital* defines, in contrast with the theoretical context of the classical economy, as that of the 'vulgar economy':[10] of the utilitarian approach to the production

---

[10] To which Marx opposes the classical economy, with which he sides. 'Adam Smith', he writes, 'got to the very heart of the matter, hit the nail on the head. This is one of his greatest scientific merits that he defines productive labour as labour which is directly exchanged with capital' (*Theories of Surplus Value,* Books I, II and III, Prometheus Books, 2000, p. 157.) As is well known, Marx, taking the analysis further, criticises and reverses the classical problematic itself by showing that what is exchanged is not work but labour power.

of utilities that he inventoried in *The Order of Things*. He does not grasp the theoretical question of the internal tension in waged work, which produces, contradictorily, use-values and surplus-value. He thus ends up circumventing the conceptuality of 'exploitation', and retranscribes it in the more general terms of 'domination', which allows its proper *materiality* to escape. He avoids the problematic of 'capitalism' as a specific social form, dynamically polarised by the search for abstract wealth. We can take this as a deficit with respect to Marx's account. But this loss ought not to hide the collateral advantage that, it seems to me, ensues from it. This *general notion of production* as the production of utilities – on this side of the 'capitalist' articulation between the production of use-value and that of surplus-value – enables Foucault to elaborate the *general concept of knowledge-power*, omnipresent in every ramification of the social order. And therein lies, in my view, his contribution to the analysis of the modern form of society, in which class power is not only that of capitalists, as owners of capital, but also that of competent-elites, as holders of social knowledge, whether or not they are situated in immediately capitalist relations.

Docility

1. As to the 'docility' of individuals thus produced as useful subjects, it qualifies not only inter-individual relations, the submission of some to others: it refers to the class relationship thus enlarged, that is, endowed with its other 'plank'. Foucault is led onto this terrain when intervening in public space, and notably when his interlocutors force him to take an entrenched

position. We could see this in his debate with Chomsky on Dutch television in November 1971 (*CF*/1–67). Here he gives us (ibid./496) a properly Marxist analysis, stated in a neo-Gramscian, post-'68 style, in the spirit of Althusser's article 'Ideology and Ideological State Apparatuses', which, published in *La Pensée* in 1970, defines 'ISAs' [ideological state apparatuses] as being the set of educational, familial, religious, etc., institutions.[11] To this list Foucault adds 'the institutions of foresight and care, such as medicine':

> It seems to me that the real task in a society such as ours is to criticise the workings of institutions, which appear to be both neutral and independent; to criticise and to attack them in such a manner that the political violence that has always exercised itself obscurely through them will be unmasked, so that one can fight against them. [...] Probably it's insufficient to say that behind the governments, behind the apparatus of the state, there is the *dominant class*; one must locate the point of activity, the places and the forms in which *its domination* is exercised. [...] Well, if one fails to recognise these points of support of *class power*, one risks allowing them to continue to exist; and to see this class power reconstitute itself, even after an apparent revolutionary process. (*CF*/41, my emphasis)

---

11 See Althusser, *Sur la reproduction,* Paris: PUF, 2011, p. 111; *The Chomsky–Foucault Debate on Human Nature,* New York/London, The New Press, 2006.

Here Foucault appears to take the term 'class' in the ordinary Marxist sense. However, he also *adds* to this concept, even if only implicitly. In short, in order to 'eliminate economic exploitation', it's not enough to win out on the terrain of institutions of 'government [...] like the administration, the police, the army or the state apparatus' (ibid., 40). The dominant class must be thwarted in all of the conditions of its existence: in the whole weft of functional institutions that form the living fabric of society. 'Docility', which is the expression of submission not to laws but to norms, is certainly expected in the process of capitalist production. Just like utility, however, it is a characteristic of the *set* of social interactions – thus understood as class relations – which are prescribed by the institutions of modern society. To sum it up: generalised docility-utility as part of productive domination.

At this point the question necessarily arises of knowing how to join the peremptory discourse of the *scholar,* who decodes the universal domination of disciplines that form useful and docile individuals, and the *political* discourse of the intellectual, who summons people to fight it. Foucault showed us how notably with his GIP (Group of Information on Prisons), which aimed at giving prisoners a voice (then, later, the ill and the mad as well). In so doing he followed in the tradition of the worker movement, which has as its mission to make the voice of the worker heard.[12] In short: indocile speech

[12] The 'worker movement' was of course continuously concerned with schooling, hospitals, etc., from a class point of view. But Foucault contributes to opening up unprecedented fronts. By way of reference, let's note that 'the common programme for government', drawn up in the years 1970–72,

against doubtful utility. So, just as Marx, in his inquiry into the working day in chapter 10 of Book 1 of *Capital*, noted the evidence of experts (inspectors, journalists, doctors, teachers), Foucault, too, mobilised key figures of knowledge-power (his friends, Badinter, Vidal-Naquet ...). Each of them affirms both the *factuality* of domination and the *potentiality* of resistance. But from where does the factuality of this potentiality proceed? In the name of what does this resistance assert itself? And in virtue of what does it manage to do so? To Chomsky's 'idealism', notable in his reference to a more just world, Foucault retorts that 'the proletariat wages war on the ruling class [...] in order to win and not because it is just' (*DE2*/503). This nevertheless leads him to the idea that what the proletariat aims at is the 'suppression [...] of class power *in general*' (my italics). Then he takes up the opposite stance: it is a matter of a 'justification in terms of power, not in terms of justice' (*DE2*/504). Notwithstanding, his argument ultimately reveals a *universalist horizon of emancipation from all class power, from class power in general*. In thus choosing his camp, Foucault makes an ultimate metastructural avowal. He does, it is true, use Nietzsche as a reference here (*DE2*/504–5): 'justice' is an historical invention, able to be used in diverse senses. But this by no means results in his excluding this notion, since his argumentation inserts it within the very same class relationship: 'anyway, the very

which, it is true, planned the abolition of the death penalty and the prohibition of police custody, does not contain a single sentence about the asylum or the prison. [Trans. – The above-mentioned 'common programme for government' was agreed by the French Communist and Socialist parties in the wake of the 1968 events and was stronger than a mere electoral alliance.]

notion of justice functions within a class society as a demand by the oppressed class and as justification on the side of the oppressors' (*DE2*/505). This expresses exactly – in accordance with the account I am putting forward – the 'amphibology' constitutive of the metastructural claim, the one that defines the above-mentioned 'essentially contested concept'. In this sense, the 'proletariat', whose spokesperson Foucault took it upon himself to be in these heroic times, necessarily puts forward, at least in the logic of struggle handed down to him, a concept of justice, of justice understood as just practice: one that aims to abolish 'class power in general'. Foucault thus highlights, in contrast with the utility-*docility* that characterises 'a society such as ours', a utility-*liberty* defined as emancipation from all class domination – a concept that includes both capitalist exploitation *and* the domination of power-knowledge.

In short, then, when addressing the concepts of (useful) production and of domination (of docility to resistance), the Foucault of *Discipline and Punish* situates himself, as have seen, in the field of class and emancipation, just as Marx did, but by broadening this field's contours and manoeuvring through it differently.

It remains for us to see if the political strategies that both approaches inspire are receptive to one another. The present research is guided by this key question. If it is raised prematurely here, the reason is that we cannot ignore that Foucault, after this cycle which began in 1968 and ended around 1976, happened subsequently to move towards an entirely other horizon of 'truth'.

4.2.2 Liberalism as productive of utility-freedom

The examination now facing us involves grasping how, only a few years later, Foucault could arrive at an identification of utility-liberty in terms of 'liberalism'. We can understand the relation between both moments more easily if we see that he not only affirms a different concept of 'production' to Marx's, but also that he has his own conception of the 'productivity' specific to power-knowledge. This idea is presented in striking fashion in the analysis on 'apparatuses of sexuality' presented in the *History of Sexuality*. So, taking this as a pivotal point, marked by the emergence of the concept of 'biopower', I now come to the second part of this decade-long journey.

The apparatus of sexuality

Despite the variety of terrains that it journeys across, Foucault's *social critique* in actual fact presents a remarkable continuity relative to the object it adopts, as well as to the negativity of domination and to the positive creativity of the power that exercises it. That is what – as much as the preceding account of discipline and subsequent account of government – his exploration of 'the apparatus of sexuality', undertaken in the years 1973–75, manifests.[13] In an interview from July 1977, he refers to Marx's able discernment behind pauperism of

---

13 See the *Lectures at the College de France* from 1973 to 1974, *Psychiatric Power,* and those of 1974–75, *Abnormal,* the lessons of which are presented in *The History of Sexuality* (1976). I leave aside these major texts, which bear more indirect links with the Marxian tradition and would merit being studied in and of themselves within a larger framework than the one I have plotted here.

'the formidable positive mechanisms' of capital. And he adds: 'I would like to do something similar [...] to discover, behind this sexual misery, what the enormous positive mechanics of power is that invests the bodies and that produces effects.'[14] The rapprochement may give cause for surprise. Foucault, we recall, had scarcely any sympathy for this power, that of wage earners, which Marx sees lying on the horizon of these 'formidable positive mechanisms'. But he is not oblivious to the 'progressist' tonalities of Marxian discourse, which he turns against the miserabilism to which another sort of Marxism attests. In contrast with the 'Marxo-Freudian' thesis about the class repression of popular sexuality, he argues that what actually occurred was an *invention* of sexuality, a placing of sex in discourse. Ancient erotics link up with private ethics. The 'flesh' of Christianity traded in prohibition in the name of morality. After, a *science* of sexuality was born, oriented towards individual and social health. This science is misled, insofar as it designates an appreciable share of sexual practices as pathological. But, in so doing, it sets up the space for a 'truth' able to be argued publicly for or against, a 'truth' that postulates a general sexual causality, open to interpretation and to interventions aiming at curing. It thus works to perform a social 'avowal' of sexuality in the spheres of justice, medicine, pedagogy, the family, and love relations. Subjects, by speaking about their sexuality, affirm their identities. There is indeed a power relation involved here: the subject speaks as a subject in the face of another's power. The

---

[14] Archives Foucault, IMEC.

law itself is constitutive of desire. But 'sex' is not to be understood in the pure juridical terms of rights, laws and punishments. It is made up of techniques of normalisation and control, of social practices that produce their object, that is, a supposedly healthy subject that is held up to critique and as such capable of resistance and rebellion.

In this context, the reference to capitalism, particularly in the 'periodisation' that Foucault sets out at the end of *The History of Sexuality*,[15] takes a positive note, in the here paradoxical sense of a class positivity. For this 'sexual science' does not aim at 'labour power'. It first spreads among the bourgeoisie: it is an affirmation of class, a mastery of class. This sexual science constitutes a 'class body', a culture of the sexed body that is part and parcel of its cultural hegemony. From the moment discipline starts repressing people for even the slightest deviations (the drunkard, the immoral, the unworthy parent), psychoanalysis comes along to liberate the bourgeoisie. Yet this all comes within a new, emergent 'biopower'. This power over life, which is a power of life in contrast with the power over death proper to classic sovereignty, amounts to a new class relationship that is exercised on the body and on the species. It is a power inherent to capitalism that runs alongside capital accumulation. In opposition to the ascetic capitalism of which Weber speaks, it marks the entry of life into history. This *positive* thematic, reprised in analogical terms at the end of

---

15 The terms cited in what follows are taken from this passage, pp. 152ff. On the relation of biopower to capitalism, see pp. 185ff.

the 1976 lectures, *Society Must Be Defended,* comes to form a major axis of Foucault's analysis of 'liberalism'.

Liberalism as positive and biopolitics

So how it is then that Foucault comes, in January 1978, to place the question of liberalism on the curriculum of his lectures at the Collège de France? It is difficult not to link the change of theoretical course to the change of political course on which he embarks at this time.[16] The 'new philosophers' embarked on a radical philosophico-political revision that came to concretion as a defence of Eastern dissidents. Until this point, the hypothesis had been widespread that there would be a slow evolution towards some form of democracy. Now, however, the ineluctable crumbling of the Soviet system loomed on the horizon, shaking to its foundations the very idea of a socialist alternative to capitalism. The USSR, fatherland of communism, came to symbolise radical evil: the society of control, repression

---

[16] On these various points, the reader may refer to the painstakingly detailed chronology drawn up by Daniel Defert (*DE1*/50–8), who notably mentions what 'many have interpreted as a crisis in his [Foucault's] reflection', towards the end of 1976. Foucault's public stances, deliberately sensational, alongside the 'new philosophers', as well as the 'second left' of J. Delors and M. Rocard, do not leave a shred of doubt. A note written by the editors, who were his friends, underlines 'his hostility to the Leninist nationalisations of the common programme' of the Left, (*DE3*/330). On his political trajectory, see notably Jose Luis Moreno Pestāna, *Foucault, la gauche et la politique,* Paris: Editions Textuel, 2010. He underscores Foucault's opposition to any alliance with the communists and his constant lack of interest in social inequalities. This position contrasts sharply with the treatment he reserved for the 'infamous men' (*EWF3*/157–75), the marginals, the wretched, the mad, vagabonds, the ill, the destitute or rebels of all sorts that are monitored and imprisoned.

and imprisonment, the unproductive society, generating subordinates. From this point on, Foucault came to take up 'liberalism', the artefact that Marx had critiqued, in positive terms. Foucault found that, just as capitalist *repression* is not the right concept to tackle the destiny of modern sexuality (which on the contrary is realised in its subjective novelty in the era of capitalism), neither does capitalist *exploitation* provide a good entry point for understanding the modern economico-political order in its historical productivity. From then on the arguments he puts forward no longer take class relations as their background, contrary to his stance at the beginning of the decade. This does not mean he abandoned his previous struggles. He remained committed on multiple fronts: prisons, hospitals, asylums, courts, homosexuality, the right to abortion, freedom in the East and elsewhere. Recognised as the social intellectual par excellence, he inspired and stimulated a whole range of subversive practices, and did so well beyond the borders of France, and notably among the Marxists of Italian operaism.[17] And yet, for his part, he had turned the page on Marxism. This was expressed in his encounters and convergence with philosophical, political and union currents that were seeking to free themselves of communism and the communists (and that would wind up on the fringes of neoliberalism). Occupying a Chair at the Collège de France meant he could take up questions with a distance and propose for analysis a historical perspective

---

17 See Marco Enrico Giacomelli, 'Ascendances et filiations foucauldi-ennes en Italie: l'operaisme en perspective', *Actuel Marx* No. 34, *Marx et Foucault,* Paris: PUF, 2004, pp. 109–122.

that did not engage him politically. Engaging him nonetheless was a decision to update 'liberalism', taken as a paradigm of modern economico-political rationality. He thus came to take up an antipodal point to Marx's and interesting problems result from this.

After studying the disciplinary techniques that emerged in the seventeenth century, and which gave rise to a certain 'political anatomy', Foucault, as we've seen, begins his considerations of what to his mind comprises the novelty of the second half of the eighteenth century: a 'biopolitics' oriented around the life of the population. This is the inaugural topic of the lectures of 1978–79. He clarifies this in his 'summary' (*EWF1*/73–9), a reflective and very dense text written after the fact. From now on, juridico-political constraints are no longer what ensure order, understood as an absence of infractions against the law, of disorder or of internal or external war, but instead a new 'art of governing' that takes aim positively at the 'public good'. Biopolitics, as we know, governs not subjects equipped with rights and duties, but a 'population', a set of living beings, partaking as such of specific forms of knowledge and know-how concerning 'health, sanitation, the birth rate, longevity and races' (*EWF1*/73). In the administrative age of the 'police', in the old sense of the term, and even more in the liberal age, this begins to bear on all the conditions of material existence: resources, production, commerce, infrastructures and urbanism. There is thus a seeming passage from a negative power, exercised 'in a negative form, that is to say, in a juridical form', to a positive power that is founded on knowledge.

The concept of 'biopolitics' in some sense gives concrete substance to that of 'power-knowledge' and defines its supposed object: a politics of life, at once normalising and productive, rational in this twofold sense. This in itself is a powerful resource for the study of power, in the era of science, in what it exercises at once on individuals and populations right down to the most intimate materiality of their bodies and largely unbeknownst to them. All research carried out into capitalism's hold on life, on the nature that bears life, can invoke him in this respect.

It will be noted, however, that this does not mean Marx is thrown out of the game. Foucault can be shown to have been unjust in his relation. On the basis of Foucault's own foregrounding of 'the adjustment of phenomena of population to economic processes', of the 'adjustment of the accumulation of men to that of capital' (*HS*/141), he believes he can reproach Marx for focusing on the analysis of class and for 'bypassing' (*STP*/79) the problems of population, dear to Malthus. Yet there is no forgetting that, in chapter 25 of Book 1 of *Capital*, 'The general law of capitalist accumulation', Marx deals at length with 'the law of population peculiar to the capitalist mode of production', and notably with the diverse categories of 'relative overpopulation' that are linked to the irregular movements of capital, to the expropriation of country dwellers, as well as with migrations, etc., up to and including 'absolute overpopulation', in which all are deprived of resources.[18] He keeps quite a distance

18 On this topic the reader may refer to Guillaume Sibertin-Blanc, 'La loi de population du capital, biopolitique d'Etat, hétéronomie de la politique de classe', in Franck Fischbach (ed.), *Relire le Capital,* Paris: PUF, 2009.

from the functional rationality that appears to announce a 'biopolitics'. And he is aptly placed to shed light on a biopolitics from below. In truth, if one wants to grasp Marx in his radical novelty as the initiator of a biopolitics from below – which is the ultimate object of his research – one must examine his entire theory of modern society from this perspective and reprise it on the basis of its constitutive concepts, those surrounding the theory of value and of surplus-value.[19]

Let us note here that the Foucauldian problematic contains uncertainties that obscure the biopolitical question it brings to light. In the last section of *History of Sexuality*, 'Right to death and power over life', in which the term *biopolitics* appears for the first time, we enter into an uncertain play between *biopolitics*, which pertains to politics, and *biopower*, which pertains to power in general. Foucault underscores the correlation between the power to make live and the power to massacre, when 'massacres have become vital' (*HS*/137). But have they not been so since the most ancient times,[20] at least in certain circumstances, the evaluation of which falls to the strongest? One is thus surprised to learn that 'the atomic situation is now at the end point of this process' (ibid.). Foucault takes up questions here that are henceforth essential, and which relate to the modern human hold over life, for which

---

[19] I take the liberty of referring again to my *Le Néolibéralisme, Un autre grand récit*, Paris: Les Prairies Ordinaires, 2016, and notably to the first chapter, 'Le corps biopolitique du Capital'.

[20] On the war of extermination in the Paleolithic era see, Alain Testard, *Avant l'histoire. L'évolution des sociétés de Lascaux à Camac*, Paris: Gallimard, 2013, pp. 498ff.

he bequeathed us invaluable concepts. But they take hold, as we have seen, only in their critical hybridisation with others.

In this regard, the best thing is no doubt to rediscover Foucault on the terrain that is most familiar to him, and on which he worked until the end of that decade: that of public medicine. But here again the connotation of *rational domination* that tends to attach to this concept of biopolitics is not necessarily a good guide. Initially oriented by concerns with the city's public hygiene, public medicine in the nineteenth century would essentially be developed as a technique of effective management and normalisation of labour power. Foucault attributes to liberalism here a movement of reform that, in actual fact, attests far more to the taking off of a nascent socialism.[21] Here again the question arises: who exercises which biopower? It seems to me that what is designated as 'biopolitics' is better able to find its place in a larger theoretical and historical context, one conceived in metastructural terms, where *diverse social forces*, from above and from below, have the *initiative*. It's on this basis – and not on that of the simple

---

[21] See Emmanuel Renault, 'Biopolitique, medicine sociale et critique du libéralisme', in *Multitudes,* No. 34, 2008, and *Souffrances sociales,* Paris: La Découverte, 2008, pp. 219–46. He shows that 'social medicine', in the forms that it takes in France and in Germany after 1848 (and from the impetus it was given by the French Revolution), does not form part of the normalising biopolitics that Foucault attributes to liberalism. On the contrary, it is affirmed as a medical activity in its own right. It submits to critique the sanitary and administrative controls then in force and ties its aims to those of a socialist transformation, which can just as easily align itself with a 'liberal' theory of right. This, I would add, in effect bears, as we have seen, the seal of 'modern amphibology'.

schema domination–resistance – that the configuration and the nature of political power in modern society can be deciphered, and that strategies can be conceived. Such is at least the thesis I shall put forward.

4.2.3 Liberalism as relation between governors and the governed

What precisely is the power that Foucault shows us under the name of 'liberalism'? Here we must once again underline the gap between Foucault's inquiry and Marx's. The latter was a theoretician of the capitalist *structure* and its historical *tendency*. As part of that structure he studies 'bourgeois society' through the *market* rationality of capitalists-in-competition and the unintentional effects (concentration of production, etc.) that ensue from it, coming to determine a historical tendency toward socialism. He takes liberalism, qua set of economic and political doctrines linked to the practices of capitalism in which society represents itself as a play of exchanges, as the object of his 'critique', correlative to his theoretical construction. Foucault has no ambition to propose any theory of the historical process of modern society. He concentrates not on a structure and its tendency but instead on a type of 'governmental practice' that is constitutive of a form of biopolitics deemed specific to that era. 'Liberalism' is not broached as a 'theory' or as an 'ideology', but as a particular form of 'political rationality' (*EWF1*/73–4).

A certain tension can nevertheless be observed in Foucault's discourse, taken as a whole, between the register of 'class' and that of 'government'. On the one hand, he presents liberalism in its relation to acts in the market and within organisation; and his words can then be marshalled, as we have seen (§2.2.2), to provide a description of modern class relationships. On the other hand, this context comes to be covered over with an articulation of socio-political space in terms of governors/governed.

On one hand, contrary to what might be expected, far from being polarised around the sole perspective of the market, whose 'law' it is supposed to respect, liberal government practises 'the subtle game of interventions and freedoms', which the 'public good' requires (*DE3*/729–30). It is of course 'anxious to have the respect of legal subjects and to ensure the free enterprise of individuals' (*EWF1*/73), however it also possesses the regulatory (that is to say *organisational*) capacity to define a general end and to arrange the means it requires. This end is not its own reinforcement (it 'breaks with the preceding 'reason of state'), but instead 'society' itself, its life, which it aims to 'maximise', in the terms of a 'maximal economy' of means (ibid.). In his study on 'The politics of health in the eighteenth century' (*DE3*/725–42), Foucault paints an impressive fresco of the *public* institutions created at this time alongside the bourgeoning market of medicine. The 'biopolitics' that they illustrate is most certainly *not that of the market.*

As we've seen (§§2.1.1–2.1.2), this is the way in which Foucault supplies what *Marx is missing.* Marx, in this sense more liberal than the liberals, proceeds, at least in his major theoretical work, as though modernity in its entirety could be thought on the basis of the market, including the 'organised form' (dating from the time of the factory) that develops in its midst and must ultimately replace it, leading to the abolition of the 'market form', and to the construction of a higher concept of united social subjectivity. More profoundly than those who since Weber have succeeded him on this path, Foucault shows that modern rationality, not only in its political content but also *in its socio-economic substance,* develops, parallel to the *market form,* in the *organised form* the ambiguous rationalities of which he strove – and in this sense his research throughout the decade shows continuity – to explore in the domains of the hospital, the prison, the school and the army, and urbanism under the aegis of forms of knowledge-power.

On the other hand, however, we see that everything that can be said to be significant about modern class *structure* and its constitutive autonomy gets referred to the tasks of a *government* in charge of an *'administrative', 'disciplinary'* and *'police' order at the same time as a 'laissez-faire' economic order.* And this liberal governmentality is exercised both in terms of that which is 'rational' and that which is 'reasonable'. As Foucault puts it, 'It is bound to inquire not just as to the best (or least costly) means of achieving its effects but also as to the possibility, and even the lawfulness, of its scheme for achieving effects' (*EWF1*/74). The liberal technology of government naturally 'does not derive' from a juridical idea; it does not presume a 'society founded on a contractual link'. But it is regulated by means of 'law' (as opposed to the adoption of particular measures), in conjunction with the 'participation of the governed [...] in a parliamentary system' (*EWF1*/77). At this point, as we see, power ceases to figure as the power of a class: it is analysed as a fact of government. With this passage from the art of punishing, educating and curing to the singular art of 'governing', it appears that it is the 'governers' who possess it, and exercise it over those they govern. *The social order, now examined through the filter of politics, has as its pivotal point the relation between governors and the governed.* The concept of 'capitalism' arranges society around the class relationship; that of 'liberalism', around the relation of government.

Foucault introduces 'governmentality' via a notion he borrows from Paul Veyne, namely that of the *pastoral*. In so doing he exhumes a line of thought and practices that first took shape in early, and notably monastic, Christianity, and which bore on the 'government of souls'. With the imperative to know each person and achieve the salvation of all, this figure ties a category of obedience in which the governor is engaged in a symmetric constraint of absolute devotion. Subject to this conduct of his conducts, the subject himself is convoked to a critique of his internal truth, to an authentic designation of self, which oscillates between voluntary subjection and resistance. In the modern era (and *only* then – a point that seems to me decisive) this figure becomes a political paradigm. This is the perspective from which Foucault grasps both the successive emergence of the administrative state and liberal government and the 'insurrections of conduct' that ensue one after the other from the era of Reforms to the time of Revolutions up to and including 1917 (*STP*/234), with a particular insistence on the case of the USSR, which is excessively pastoral (*STP*/204). It could be asked what motivates the emergence of this concept, which nothing in Foucault's foregoing research would seem to announce. It constitutes, so it seems to me, the medium that will enable him to take leave of the philosophico-political tradition to which Marxism is attached: that which in the last resort defines the state as a class state. The 'pastoral' – this is its epistemological *raison d'être* – makes it possible to tackle the question of politics no longer on the basis of the relation between classes, that is as the question of the state (of the class state), but instead *on the basis of the relation between governors and the governed*, which is to say, on the question of Government. Beyond the attention that he gives to its productive or totalitarian potentialities, what Foucault does is to transport us from a world structured into classes, involving the dominant and the dominated, to a world arranged between governors and the governed.

The concept of 'pastoral' designates 'government' as a transitive social process, which permits an analysis of social and political rationality in terms of the 'art of governing'. Corresponding to it is a certain conception of freedom: 'Freedom is never anything other – but this is already a great deal – than an actual relationship between governors and governed *(BB/63)*. When servitude and freedom are decided purely in relation to 'government', state power leads us to forget the power of class. One could not be more 'liberal'. At this point of his lectures, or of his discourse – the difference is not easy to see – Foucault 'rids himself of Marxism'. But it is difficult not to inquire into the critical withdrawal that is thus performed between the beginning and the end of 1970.

4.2.4 'Governmentality' as
against self-government

The 'pastoral' and 'governmentality' in actual fact return us to the figure of 'civil society'. This enables Foucault to bypass the *revolutionary* problematic of right considered on the basis of its 'origin', to rid himself of the 'theoretical and juridical problem of the original constitution of society' (*BB*/308). Foucault stressed the limits of his research: the idea was to engage in only one 'possible level of analysis – that of "governmental reason"' (*BB*/322). He saw in this duality state/civil society a 'form of schematisation proper to a particular technology of government' (*BB*/319). Nevertheless this *schema*, to adopt one of Marx's terms, does form the 'guiding thread' of his historical inquiry. The 'liberal' governmentality that he frames is founded on the supposed virtue of the market.[22] As a result, this yields a paradoxical 'liberalism with a human face'. The very thinker who had declared the end of humanism and buried

---

22 Citing *The Birth of Biopolitics,* Céline Spector stresses that Foucault's recourse to Ferguson explicitly puts him in the footsteps of Hayek: 'It's Hayek who said, some years ago: We need a liberalism that is a living thought. [...] It is up to us to create liberal utopias [...]' (*BB*/218–19). She suggests that the 'radical critique' can well be, 'without wanting or knowing it', inverted into a 'liberal critique', in the manner of 'P. Rosanville, P. Manent, M. Gauchet and above all F. Ewald' ('Foucault, les Lumières et l'histoire: l'émergence de la société civile', in *Lumières,* No. 8. Bordeaux, 2007, pp. 190–1). I. Garo shows convincingly how Foucault, without ever saying that liberalism is 'true', comes to inscribe himself in liberalism (p. 151). To which it must be added that this does not prevent him from proclaiming, again in 1978, that 'a really socialist governmentality [...] must be invented' (*BB*/94). It remains to be known, of course, what might be meant by 'socialism' here.

the figure of man here has that of *homo* reappear. Following on from Hume, he intends to confront the 'formal heterogeneity', the radical division between the *homo juridicus,* the subject of right, and *homo oeconomicus,* the subject of interest *(BB/276).* The liberal solution consists in identifying the former with the latter, as personified by market man, a figure thus recognised as the elementary link of the juridical order. This takes us outside the disjunctive register of *Discipline and Punish,* in which the imaginary (the formal, appearance, the ideal ...) of the juridical fiction is contrasted with the reality of the disciplinary order. At issue this time is the *scission* between the economic and the juridico-political. This is exactly the scission, *die Spaltung,* of which Marx spoke,[23] between the 'bourgeois' and the 'citizen', and for which he sought a *political* way out by establishing an economy that would be organised among all in democratic fashion. Foucault, conversely, shows us how liberalism surmounts it through 'indexing' the order of right to the economic order of the market. That is precisely what he defines as the performance of 'liberalism', nevertheless holding in rhetorical suspense both the question of its legitimacy and that of its status in reality.[24]

---

[23] On this split between 'the political state and bourgeois civil society' (to use Marx's terms), a central theme of *The Jewish Question,* see Solonge Mercier-Josa's rigorous philological analysis in *Entre Hegel et Marx,* Paris: L'Harmattan, 1999.

[24] However, it is notable here that, in contrast with his works on the asylum, sexuality or the prison, Foucault does not bring to light any particular 'apparatus', strategy or tactic. He ultimately does no more than adopt the discourse of liberals, taking up the ambiguous position of the observer.

Foucault, moreover, is in fact left facing a problem of the origin: it is a matter of knowing on what basis one can legitimately ground, or conceive of, an order of right. And he answers this question by producing *another* origin, an originary presupposition, according to which there *must* and will always be governors and the governed, an eternal origin … The governors are tasked with managing certain historical necessities – in this case, those of the market – of significance for the rationality of our time.

The question arises, however, if the *modern* political question can be reduced in this way to one of a negotiation, albeit antagonistic, between governors and the governed. Is the issue not rather (notably since Hobbes) about the modern subject governing itself? Or else, can an art of governing, in the modern era, *appear* otherwise than as a mode of transaction between subjects that claim to govern *themselves?* The invariable retort is that rather from setting out from some such *claim*, it is more realistic to begin with *what is:* from the fact that a 'government' necessarily exists. Indeed it is also possible on this basis to think through the various forms of *resistance*. And such is the end that Foucault successfully pursued. But can we follow this inclination of his? Can the true radicality of the modern political problem be presented in these terms? Is our *claim to govern ourselves* – from which an entire lineage of political philosophers sets out, via Rousseau and Kant to Marx – *an unreal thing,* as it were?[25] The metastructure, in which this claim

---

25 It is notable that this question is avoided in Foucault's discourse notably insofar as this 'we' is regularly replaced by a 'one'. Page after page, he

is inscribed, has a transactional existence only, a claim-related existence. It only ever exists as *instrumentalised* in the modern class *structure* that is constituted through the *double mediation*, that of the two 'class factors' of *market and organisation*. But this *instrument* is one that class struggle never ceases to seize hold of, always anew. Indeed, it is on this basis that the revolutionary process immanent to modernity has conceived itself. Foucault's critical realism makes a distribution: *at the top* there is an art of governing, played out entirely in strategies; and *at the bottom*, practices of resistance. Is the power from below, which is that of the multitude, reducible to this capacity to resist which supposedly fuels productive domination?

In sum, Foucault is led by turns to sympathise with all forms of self-management (just as formerly Marx was filled with enthusiasm for the Russian commune), *against* hierarchical, bureaucratic organisation, but also to adopt the liberal watchword according to which there also tends to be 'too much' government. Marx claimed that the more the market was enforced, the more violent governing became. This is because the state is first and foremost not civil society; it crowns the class relationship, the contradictions of which it concentrates. In Foucault's view, on the contrary, twentieth-century liberalism (i.e. ordo-liberalism and the Chicago

---

reveals to us the genesis of 'our modern political rationality'. Notable also is the fact that the question of democracy, evoked in terms of the 'parliamentary system' in the lecture course summary (*EWF* 1/73) for the years 1978–79, is paradoxically absent from the lectures themselves, as if it was not essential to 'our modern rationality'.

School) increasingly radicalised the 'critique of the irrationality specific to the excess of governmentality' (*EWF1*/77), to which Nazism, Communism and also the Keynesian New Deal attest. The (Marxian) idea that some *irrationality* can also attach itself to a capitalist market dynamic, and affect it with a growing coefficient of unproductiveness in terms of 'use-values', does not surface in Foucault's account. This does not mean it does not cross his mind. It is evidently present in the background. But it is not theoretically invested in his critical work.[26] It is not his object of research.

At this point a number of questions arise. To what point does Foucault commit himself exactly by adopting this use of the term 'liberalism', by which this tradition of thought and practice designates itself? To what extent does he adopt the claim tied to it, namely that of the co-naturality of economic liberalism and political liberalism? What part, in all this, belongs to social theory and what part to the interpretative reprise of a dominant class discourse? What is, in his view, the degree or the sort of reality that belongs to 'civil society', which he calls on us – notably in his last course on the topic, held on 4 April 1979 – to consider as a simple 'transactional reality', as a 'governmental technology'? That is to say, as pertaining to a *practical* conceptuality, which it would be thought a conceptual

---

26 Frédéric Lebaron shows, however, that Foucault's linking-up with union and political movements, which announced the rise of neoliberalism, is accompanied by a tendency to oppose the dismantling of certain social gains. See his article 'De la critique de l'économie à l'action syndicale', in Didier Eribon (ed.) *L'Infréquentable Michel Foucault*, Paris, EPEL, 2001, pp. 157–64.

edifice with the social structure as its object could help us to decipher. And what, ultimately, is that 'art of governing' in which the secret equilibrium between the market and its regulation is carried out? Who are the agents that a coherent nominalism might identify as exercising this art? How do they go about reproducing themselves? What relations do they entertain with what Foucault readily designates as the 'bourgeoisie', and sometimes also as the 'dominant class'? In his work it is difficult to find replies to these questions, especially as they are not raised, even though the account irresistibly elicits them.

Despite all these ambiguities, which accumulate along the last phase of his journey, Foucault did not cease to breathe life into the wind of resistance. Nothing can make us forget the powerful analytical and critical impetus that flows, notably, from his elaboration of the concept of knowledge-power, the beginning of a profound renewal of the very idea of modern society. It is therefore not prohibited to reprise the heritage he bequeathed us, together with Marx's, and the strategy from below that each of them sought to promote.

ELEMENTS OF CONCLUSION: A STRATEGY FROM BELOW

This brings us back, then, to the 'contradiction among the people' from which we set out. It is of course well known that property and knowledge are always linked in some way. But the concepts that enable us to decipher the two factors of modern class power here pertain to heterogeneous theoretical approaches, which tend to seek support in antagonistic philosophies and suggest different versions of human emancipation. Among those who find inspiration in Marx or in Foucault, respectively, it is therefore not at all easy to agree a strategic perspective.

MARX'S STRATEGIES

In his historical works, Marx analyses the strategies and tactics of the bourgeoise and its different fractions. However in his major theoretical work, he devotes himself to founding, at the same time as a critical analysis of capitalist society, the principles of a *strategy of the proletariat*. Those who have aligned with him, from Lenin to Mao, from Jaurès to Gramsci, from Castro to many others, without forgetting those who have worked to promote socialism within capitalism, have followed him along this path. The forms proposed have been as diverse as the historical conditions faced. But the general line advanced has remained the same: it is a matter, on the basis of the power that industrial concentration gives the working class, of gathering together all workers for the purpose of establishing an economy that is subject no longer to the 'law of the market', but instead to a democratic organisation controlled by the people concerned. Socialism certainly aligns itself with the international, but it is become reality in a new form of nation state. With hindsight, we are better able today to gauge the revolutionary impact of the communist movement of the first half of the twentieth century throughout the world – and notably its role in the metamorphosis of ancient societies that were subjugated for some while by imperialisms – but also the limits of this historical experience.[1] In 'real socialism', the knowledge-power of cadres of organisation most often gave rise to a new dominant class and a regime of hegemony fated to deadly contradictions. Or else, as in China, it has finally connected with capitalist power. As to 'socialism under capitalism', carried out as an alliance between knowledge-power and the fundamental class, it also profoundly marked the course of world history for thirty years of the postwar period. But it entered into a fatal crisis as the 1980s came

---

1 For an assessment, see Göran Therborn, 'Class in the 21st Century', *New Left Review*, November-December 2012.

upon us. Financial capital, which has never ceased to give new importance to old projects, has finally managed, harboured by technological (including the development of digital technology) and geopolitical conditions (virtually unpaid work and an availability of wealth to pillage on the periphery), to impose a neoliberal hegemony on a global scale, neutralising former prospects for a national and social state. The Right and the Left have come to figure as variants of the same politics: a challenge for those who continue to think that we will be unable to break the dominant class without an alliance between the (hegemonic) people and knowledge-power.

FOUCAULT'S STRATEGIES

Foucault was a social actor, an inspirer of struggles that often proved fecund. In the manner of Marx, he intervened both in theory and in practice. Throughout the 1970s, the terms 'strategy' and 'tactics', often used in tandem, recurred regularly in his discourse in connection with the idea of class struggle. They concerned, by turns, the dominant and the dominated. But the concept of 'strategy' is more immediately connected to that of 'domination' (*DE3/94ff*) and is therefore ascribed to the apparatuses of the 'bourgeoisie' operative in the diverse institutional fields of prison, law, education, health, psychiatry and sexuality. Foucault does not forget the economic dimension. For the concepts of knowledge-power also hold for the analysis of labour relations. But the overall process, in which knowledge-power and (capitalist) property-power are articulated, remains outside his field, as does the strategic challenge corresponding to it. All in all, the Foucauldian strategy and the Marxist strategy turn their backs on each other: each of them sets up on its adopted front and ignores the other. Marx, who reasons in terms of social *structures,* cannot immediately get to strategies. As we've seen, he defines the class relationship not as being between two substantially constituted social groups, but instead as a divisor, as a structural process of division that gives rise to more or less lasting groupings (the 'industrial working class', the mining patronat, etc.). The 'class consciousness' of these groups is affirmed in accordance with the technological transformations that determine variable strategic opportunities, situated at the juncture of tendencies and conjunctures. Foucault, who, as we've seen, grasps social space in terms of *apparatuses,* thinks at the more *immediately concrete* register of powers and domination, that is in terms of 'strategy'. He depicts a dominant class that is self-aware in the implementation of its apparatuses of power. The bourgeoisie of the nineteenth century, he writes, developed 'an absolutely conscious, organised, and deliberate strategy' (*FL*/149).[2] A return to the archives that conserve its memory helps us to understand better its present-day strategies (its arsenal of 'laws made by some and imposed on others' (ibid.), and to elaborate tactics in return – for which Foucault proposes his 'box of tools' (ibid.).

---

2 Its penal system is made up of 'perfectly calculated, mastered strategies of power' (*SPu*/240).

He does not ignore the fact that the proletariat also finally arrived (among others, under the influence of Marxism) at a certain 'self-awareness', and that it sought, over the course of a long century, to elaborate an opposing and historically significant strategy. But this experience was ultimately one that aroused little enthusiasm in him. Rather it incited him to reject in advance any idea of putting forward an overall strategy in the name of emancipation. The bourgeoisie waged a class struggle, but did not – this is the argument of the 'war of races' – adopt the mad and dangerous claim to attempt to put an end to it. For his part, Foucault works at furnishing the dominated with *tactical* elements for counterattacks, for their counteroffensives. His intention is assuredly informed by the idea that resistance is summoned to translate into an advance; and that, on the diverse fronts of rights for prisoners, the mad, women, foreigners, homosexuals, etc., 'new strategies' have to be invented (*DE3*/265–7). He even asserts, against a certain leftist anarchism, the necessity for an articulation between such strategies (*PK*/129–30). But he recoils from naming the social subject that would be its bearer. He disqualifies in advance those who claim to be charged in its name with a *strategic mission*. The 'politics of truth' – which Foucault places, as we've seen, under the aegis of 'philosophy' – aims to provide sectoral struggles with an overall direction. It thereby outlines a framework for a strategy of emancipation. But in so doing it does not define any unified historical subject, or, as 'the bourgeoisie' once was, any social force bearing a strategy without strategist (and whose legatee the proletariat could present itself as being). Foucault grasps it in its twofold identity as capitalist power – always in the background of his work – and as knowledge-power, which, as the immediate object of his investigation, is a productive social power. As to the resistance that this class domination encounters, he certainly thinks of it as a *power* to resist, but he does not come up with any historically defined, *positive concept* of such 'power' – one that could indeed signify the ultimate avowal of a subalternity. And one is led to ask why it is so difficult to conceive the strategy from below, which Gramsci, in reference to Machiavelli, called the 'modern prince'. Could it be condemned to the pure 'labour of the negative'?

The Foucauldian discourse of 'resistance' refers notably to a conceptuality that is atemporal rather than historically defined. This is how he retranslates a notion, taken from Hegel's discourse about the society of his time, namely that of the 'plebs', which he places in a *general* register in order to designate the 'permanent, ever silent target of apparatuses of power' (*PK*/137–8). It is a reactive target. There is thus, he says, 'some plebeness' or 'plebeian quality': 'in bodies, in individuals, in the proletariat, in the bourgeoisie' (ibid., 138). Power relations here constantly hit their limits. Their undertakings arouse in the partner an endless 'movement to get free of them'. Here we have some sort of vitalist feature, a fact of human nature, a capacity inscribed in the body. The living being, as living being, is always free. Similarly, he says, with the freedom of the slave, so long as he is not in irons: there is always a capacity to escape (*EWF3*/342). When he talks about this 'permanent provocation', to be understood as 'both reciprocal incitation and struggle' (ibid.), Foucault does not only have in mind a particular antagonistic social configuration, but instead an agonism specific to the human condition.[3] As a challenge to Marxism's supposed orientation around the illusory horizon of a reconciled society, he claims to find in 'Nietzschean genealogy' a 'strategic method concerning struggle', which Marxism is missing (DE3/605–6). Struggle has been there since the dawn of time; and war is the 'cipher of peace'. However, it remains to be asked whether, by holding to the anthropological register of a supposed human nature – whereas he intends to perform a *history* of political reason – he is able to account for a *historically defined* capacity from below, and to conceive of something like a strategy *for today,* which would supply tactics and counterattacks with a horizon of historical universality. If the aim is to understand modern class struggle according to its own logics and conditions, ought one not to look, in the manner of Marx, for some such revolutionary-strategic principle within the form of modern society itself?

---

[3] With Judith Butler (*The Psychic Life of Power*, Stanford, CA: Stanford University Press, 1997), we may see in this a version of the *turning back on oneself* by which the subject emerges. This confronts us with a certain problematic of internalisation of the law imposed on the subject, which at once accepts it and attaches to it, but attaches to itself to the point that it becomes capable of denying this acceptance-attachment. It is a living subject of the law, outside of defined time. Guillaume Le Blanc underlines that the reversal thus suggested appeals, in the terms of a universal anthropological discourse, to a 'desire to live', which 'brings with it vital polarities that are not made totally clear'. See *Actuel Marx,* No. 36, 2004, p. 59.

PROVOCATION AND INTERPELLATION

The argumentation put forward here in order to treat this question is part of a research programme most aptly referred to as 'metastructural'. Deciphering the 'structure' on the basis of the amphibological presuppositions that it produces, it seeks to reprise Marx's theorisation from a higher point of abstraction. As I see it, it is only at this 'altitude' that a relay between Marx and Foucault can take place.

We know well the initial 'flick of the fingers' by which the theoretical machinery of *Capital* is set in motion. The first chapter posits the notion that the value of commodities is determined by the time necessary to produce them.[4] When labour power, through the institution of the wage system, functions as a commodity, the worker must work longer than the time implied in the production of goods that procures him his wage, goods through which he reproduces himself. This is indeed the condition on which he is called upon. Through this surplus labour, he produces the surplus value that valorises the capital. But this operation is carried out strictly within a *market* framework, since labour power was bought at its value, which by definition is measured in terms of wages. The conceptuality involved here is certainly problematic; it has to answer to

---

[4] The remainder of *Capital* explains why these commodities are not exchanged at their value, but at prices that differ from it. It is therefore advisable to avoid hasty annoyance with this 'theory of value', to which Marx's account attributes a defined place: at the beginning of theory and not at its term.

an endlessly recurrent tide of objections and examinations and define rigorously the space of truth proper to it and its limits.[5] Let's dwell a moment on this formal aspect: *capitalism is understood as an instrumentalisation of market rationality.* From then on, if it is true, as the institutionalist economy says, that 'rational coordination at the social level' contains two primary modalities, namely *market* and *organisation,* then these latter are to be similarly considered as being socially *instrumentalisable.* We are then – with reference to the great analytic traditions of political philosophy and sociology – capable of understanding that these two mediations constitute the economic face of relations between each person and between all, the other face of which is juridico-political. This is what I have designated as the 'metastructural grid'. It can be concluded from this that the dominant class is not only that of capitalists: it presents two poles, one of property-power on the market and one of knowledge-power in organisation. We saw how an investigation of Foucault's work lends substance to the argument. The conditions of an encounter at the summit thus come to take shape.

But, if one wants to tackle the problem of 'resistance', concerning which the Foucauldian analysis, in its anthropological recess, leaves us unsatisfied, we must climb higher still in our theoretical construction. Both *rational-reasonable* 'mediations' can only be declared such to the extent that they

---

[5] I take the liberty of referring here to my *Explication et reconstruction du Capital.*

are presented as conveyors of understanding between free, equal and rational beings in the *immediation* of communicational discourse: in the last resort, 'one person = one voice' in a state order that rules on the claims of the market and of organisation. At least such is the *modern fiction,* which is expressed in the official discourse of liberty/equality/freedom: power-property claims these latter are assured by the 'free market', knowledge-power by the elaboration of 'concerted planning' between all. This discourse, which cannot be rejected by someone without their falling into contradiction, is the site of a *disagreement,* immanent to the modern class relationship, between those who declare from above that these demands are satisfied, insofar as it is *hic et nunc* possible, and those who proclaim from below that they must be *hic et nunc* fulfilled. This is the point at which modern class struggle is declared between those whose privileges (of property and knowledge) are reproduced in the reiteration of the structural mechanism and those whose horizon is their abolition. This 'reciprocal incitation', which Foucault presents as the principle of an *anthropological* agonism, ceaselessly renewed, here finds its *historical* determination.

The metastructural approach thus reprises in nominalist and historically circumstantial terms[6] 'the interpellation' that

6 Interpellation therefore refers us to the 'modern' form of society. It is clear that a theory of modernity is entailed here. I again take the liberty of referring to my *l'Etat-monde,* one of the goals of which is to show – using the same set of concepts employed in the present work – that modernity is not to be confounded with the 'West': it emerges in diverse places and in diverse times.

Althusser cites. But it correlates two antithetical imperatives: 'submit yourself' and 'rise up!' Interpellation is incitation, antagonistic incitation, disagreement. In the modern class context, singular persons interpellate others, who are presumed free, equal and rational by the exchange-sharing of a common discourse. Interpellation is nothing other than an amphibological inter-interpellation of class. All agents intersect with one another here, in positions of class. Foucault speaks of 'permanent provocation'. However, this is never the same at all times. Interpellation from the top down takes the form of communication that strives for effects of domination via material-institutional networks. Such, it will be said, is politics eternal. But politics plays out differently as soon as it makes claims to freedom and equality among all. The one who is interpellated as free, equal and rational is so, moreover, only because he has already risen up as such and declared himself such – throughout the course of, as Marx puts it, 'a secular struggle'. From this point on one cannot instrumentalise reason without its being summoned positively and multiply in opposition to forms of domination. The figure of a subject from below here begins to emerge. However, this does not yet define the strategy that would be proper to it.

STRATEGY AND HEGEMONY

If we are to pursue this path, the idea that there is a 'strategy of the bourgeoisie' must first be deconstructed. At issue here, to be sure, is an epistemological obstacle that hides the essential fact that, in the modern era, diverse strategies from above are possible. The reason for this is that the privileged class is an articulation of *two* social forces (capitalists/competent-elites), which are certainly in league with one another, but can also potentially enter into disagreement. Corresponding to these two poles are two types of distinct privileges, which open to those who hold them different modes of reproduction and of accumulation of their powers, and therefore different strategic perspectives: the great alienist doctors and urbanists about whom Foucault speaks, the high functionaries, judges, and so on – these figures do not spontaneously share the same horizon of power as owners of capital. *In modern society, there are indeed two classes, but the class struggle is a three-way game, because the privileged class comprises two distinct forces, founded on two distinct types of socially reproducible privileges.* The 'bourgeois' moment (1750–1930 – a basic point of reference) comprises their relative convergence at the top: these are the historical limits within which the notion that the bourgeoisie has 'a strategy' seems legitimated. Subsequently, with pressure from below and in the wake of an immense uprising, of a social upheaval that traverses all continents – and while other social formations were emerging in other systemic contexts – what came to light, in the old western centre, was an alliance, very diverse in kind and in degree, between the pole of competency and the fundamental class. The national strategies of the 'social state', whose future had seemed assured, were then asserted. The 1980s – and above I have tried to identify the conditions of this reversal – saw the triumph of a neoliberal strategy, now relatively free of the specific influence of competent-elites, the higher level of which especially has tended to go into the service of financial capital. The voraciousness of 'Finance' now sets the tone and has radicalised the strategy of abstraction that Marx defined as specific to capital, namely the accumulation of surplus-value, regardless of its consequences for humans, cultures and nature. The 'bourgeoisie' of which Marx and Foucault spoke is no longer current: it represented merely a temporary configuration. Such is, at least, the guiding thread of a metastructural history of 'regimes of hegemony',[7] understood on the basis of this variable game of alliance and confrontation across different phases of modern times between the three primary social forces constitutive of any society, which, however, come face to face in the last resort.

In short, if the powers of modern society are so diverse and variable, it is because they are not constituted in the fortress of essentially one and only one privileged class, but in the confrontation between social forces that are situated at its two poles. They are structured in the endlessly renewed games of resistance and initiative, of ascendency and disengagement, of alliance and compromise that are formed together with those below, who are never completely devoid of power either. They are rooted and criss-cross each other in the diversity of functions and dimensions of social existence. They rest on 'positions' in the order of property and social organisation, the

---

[7] See my *Le Néolibéralisme, Un autre grand récit*, Paris: Les Prairies Ordinaires, 2016, esp. Chapter 4, 'Repériodiser les temps modernes'.

privileges of which are unequally distributed among its diverse bodies, groups and individuals. On this basis it is possible to envisage – but only by resetting it each time in the conjunctural configuration of the world-system – the question of a strategy from below.

THE DISPERSED ORDER OF
STRATEGY FROM BELOW

The principle of the thing might well seem limpid. In its naïve simplicity, concerning the abstract context of this 'modern structure' with two dominant but heterogeneous poles, a strategy from below – let's call it 'metastructural' – would aim at a collective reappropriation of the market and of organisation, which in the last instance constitute the forms of our common social rationality, and which are both co-instrumentalised as part of modern class domination. In other terms, it would aim at an emancipation of class relations through a popular assimilation of both these 'mediations', which would neutralise them as class factors. Its horizon is to aim at control of the market through organisation (which is 'socialism') and control of organisation through immediate discourse, equally shared by all (which is 'communism' or radical democracy). In short, it is the control of socialism itself by communism. This is how the logic of the struggle for emancipation from class relations would be defined (without forgetting, that social emancipation does not reduce to this – we will return to this point): the construction of the *unity* of the fundamental class, which is a condition of its hegemony over the pole of competent-elites as part of an *alliance* against capitalists. Break the unity of the dominant class and abolish capitalist existence. This is to be done without ever forgetting that the alliance partner, the competent-elite, is above all a class adversary and as such is *to be surpassed* [*surclasser*] as such – in order precisely that it becomes a partner in this joint combat. This 'strategy' does not promise anything. It is merely affirmed in the manner of an essential axiom. People will say that such an abstraction does not merit the name of strategy. Its simple statement however – and this is what justifies it – enables a better identification of the obstacles that stand in the way of popular emancipation. More precisely, it enables them to be read in the mirror of the three axes of this confrontation.

Capitalist power, in fact, insofar as its end is 'abstract wealth' or surplus-value, strikes *randomly,* wherever the occasion arises to make a profit. Finance has its strategy; each hedge fund has its tactics and swoops whenever its prey becomes vulnerable. What, at the summit, is an expert strategy of financial capital – which is *organised* to the extent that it is concentrated, with the aim, ideologically proclaimed, of engaging in the *programmed* dismantling of all institutions of the social-national state, or with the aim of controlling entire branches of production – is expressed, at the base, as a *disorganised* destruction. The famous 'creative destruction' is predatory as well. It pounces on its scattered prey. The impact points are also those on the basis of which revolts emerge, from which class rage feeds strategies from below. Just as the *random* blows of capitalism arise in dispersed fashion, so, too, do replies to it. These replies can mobilise only by justifying themselves in the name of principles and norms able to be adopted by everyone. Struggle from below only triumphs by asserting itself as global. But it advances only by breaking up onto a thousand dispersed fronts.

Knowledge-power, as Foucault also stressed, exists only in the form of a multiplicity of distinct powers, of specific 'apparatuses' situated at the juncture of diverse kinds of functional demand and forms of knowledge. From this follow so many struggles of emancipation, conducted not against *power,* but against particular *powers.* And not 'against the main enemy', but against the 'immediate enemy', who is hidden in the dispersion of functions of the organisation of social life. That is, 'a whole series of power networks that traverse bodies, sexuality, the family, attitudes, forms of knowledge [and] techniques' and maintain a relation with this 'meta-power' as conditioning and conditioned (*DE3*/151). It is very much a matter of *class* power, which is reproduced structurally in a class *relationship* that transcends *relations* between individuals. But such power is exercised on singular beings in all the facets of their existence. And it is from the abyss of singularities that collective practices of emancipation must emerge that are meaningful for all.

As to the fundamental class, it can only be envisaged concretely in its relation to gender and 'race' relations, themselves also connected to the configurations of the world-system. Abstractly considered in the limits of this study – on class structure – it appears prey to two modes of division.

The vertical dimension has been raised: its metastructural, three-way fractionising. Three 'fractions' take shape in accordance with their relations to the two mediations/factors of class. Market and organisation still function as 'instruments' of the class relationship that have sway over everyone. But they do so differently depending on the relative predominance of one or the other: a hierarchical relation (public sector wage earners), a market relation (self-employed individuals in production and trade) or a more pronounced interference between the two (private sector wage earners). Class confrontation always plays out on both tableaus – market (wages, etc.) and organisation (employment conditions, etc.) – in accordance with modalities that vary from one fraction to the other. From below, this process entails a dynamic that is incessantly re-implemented, the aim of which is to reappropriate these 'instruments', to turn them into the elements of controlled coordination from below. The progress of this dynamic is measured against the 'gains' recorded, which have in common with 'privileges' (those of property-power and of knowledge-power) the fact that they exist as such only insofar as they incorporate the principle of their reproduction. Typically: norms of wages, employment, recognised qualification classifications, etc.. But the agendas of these diverse fractions, private and public, self-employed and employees, are always already out of sync, such that the idea that the 'children of the people' co-belong to one and the same 'popular class' remains highly counterintuitive. Indeed the task of theory is to show both what separates them and what unites them, whether or not they are waged, or work in the public or private sectors. This is what the metastructural grammar of the 'mediations' must serve to do.

At the same time, this outlines the *second, horizontal division* of the fundamental class. For its advances are of course unequal and depend upon the force relations established historically in diverse professional contexts. Insofar as an alliance between competency and the people prevailed in the crucible of the social-national state, the tendency to a unification of conditions was buoyed by popular participation in this regime of hegemony, and thus by organisational dispositions pertaining to the law, that is to say, by the critical staging of a certain universality. With neoliberalism, which neutralises all national-statist authority as much as it can, the gap widens between those able to enforce the 'gains', through the effect of accumulated corporate power, and those excluded from them or prevented from gaining access to them, who are reduced to the status of the invisible. One cannot confound 'gains' and 'privileges'. One cannot, as people on various sides are proposing today, analyse this new social order on the basis of the gap separating the privileged, able to participate in 'agreement', and the others, who are more or less excluded from it, relegated to 'dis-agreement'. This is because this gap, which is obvious, pertains to a less immediately legible but more profound division, which is to say that class division which defines modern society in all its scope, contradictions, dynamics and horizons, as a battlefield. The metastructural approach to class provides an analytic operator, a principle of explanations and interpretations. However, the priorities and the perspective of a metastructural strategy are defined and fixed by the voice of those 'without part', qua bearers of the universal that the people, as dispersed and divided, is always lacking. For the voice of those 'without part' alone is adequate to the critical claims of modernity.

BEYOND CLASS HORIZONS

Hitherto we have remained – as was the object of the present research – within the abstract framework of an expanded 'class structure' containing both Marx and Foucault. The edifice has been refounded on the concept of 'the instrumentalisation of reason', in turn leading us to formulate a strategic principle of emancipation and to identify the obstacles to it. This fine abstraction must nonetheless be deemed insufficient and even misleading when taken alone. For modern society is this and also something further, which can only be mentioned briefly here.[8]

Domination, exploitation and modern violence present another dimension: not one of 'structural' class relations, but of the world in its geographical, 'systemic' whole, insofar as it is made up of distinct territorial societies, ideally in the form of nation states. This relation of domination does not pertain to the appropriation of means of production or of forms of knowledge-power by a dominant class, but to the appropriation of territories by ethnic or state communities.

---

8 This is the topic of *L'Etat-monde*.

The pertinent concepts here belong to the notion of 'world-system' and cannot be referred back to an *instrumentalisation* of reason: the thematics of racism, which are founded on reason's *negation* in those that one oppresses and who thus are cast outside modern interpellation, provide an illustration of this. They show a different global (systemic and not structural) dimension of modernity and, within it, the space of the colony and the postcolony. Neither Marx nor Foucault traces any path for emancipation from the yolk of the world-system. Internationalism itself is only a lateral treatment of a question that has to be tackled head-on. At issue is not only the domination of peoples-territories over others. Nor even of centres over peripheries, nor of their interpenetration. For what is in question is the relation of appropriation between a territory and a people that lays claim to being a state community. And it is also the modern 'republic', with which the nation state aligns itself, medium of liberty for oneself and of oppression for the other, that must be 'emancipated'. We are yet to find out what that larger horizon is.[9]

Nor does domination in respect of sex – taken in the materialist feminist sense as 'social relations of sex' – have the least to do with any such 'instrumentalisation of reason'. It attests not to the reversal of a natural-reasonable complementarity, but instead to a force relation between the sexes, which, historically constituted and recurrent, is legible in the

---

[9] The problems of an overall bottom-up strategy are the subject of Chapter 8 of *L'Etat-monde*, 'Au terme territoriale de la modernité: l'imbroglio du world-Système et de l'Etat-monde'.

history of forms of knowledge-power elaborated by Foucault and in the economico-political trajectories sketched by Marx. If these diverse struggles are able to reach their goal, it will be within the mirror of universal rights rather than that of 'difference'. They succeed only as stakeholders of the common cause. But they are simultaneously bound up in a wholly other temporality, pertaining to an entirely different measure of urgency and immediate demand. And this applies *a fortiori* to any amalgamation of singularities at the junction of these diverse motives for emancipation, whether they relate to sex, class or 'race'.

In short, the histories and agendas of emancipation do not come together to form a grand narrative. However, interpellation is universal and nothing escapes, at least not in principle, from being communicated among all humans. Humanity now confronts itself as a perishable species, a simple link of the life that bears it. Discourses apt to integrate unity and diversity, contradiction and solidarity, invention of the future and respect for nature are not theories. They are collective creations, cultural and political ones, which are forged through struggles and experiences in the day-to-day, part of a diverse memory always and ever under construction. Theoretical work can nevertheless participate.

REFERENCES

WORKS OF MARX

Capital, Vol. 1, trans. Ben Fowkes, London: Penguin Classics, 1992.

Capital, Vol. 2, trans. David Fernbach, London: Penguin Classics, 1992.

Capital, Vol. 3, trans. David Fernbach, London: Penguin Classics, 1991.

A Contribution to the Critique of Political Economy. London: Lawrence and Wishart, 1971.

Critique of the Gotha Programme, trans. Joris de Bres, in *The First International and After*, London: Verso, 2010.

Grundrisse, translation and foreword by Martin Nicolaus, London: Penguin Classics, 1993. Published in German as *Grundrisse der Kritik der politischen Ökonomie*, Berlin: Dietz Verlag, 1974.

Marx-Engels-Werke, Berlin: Karl Dietz Verlag, 1956–1990.

WORKS OF FOUCAULT
published during his lifetime

Discipline and Punish: The Birth of the Prison, trans. Alan Sheridan, London: Penguin, 1991. First published as

Surveiller et punir: Naissance de la prison, Paris: Editions Gallimard, in 1975.

History of Sexuality, Vol. 1, translated by Robert Hurley, London: Penguin, 1990. First published in 1976 as *La Volonté de savoir*, Paris: Gallimard.

Power/Knowledge: Selected Interviews and Other Writings 1972–1977, ed. Colin Gordon, trans. Colin Gordon, Leo Marshall, John Mepham and Kate Soper, London: Harvester Wheatsheaf, 1980.

published posthumously

Abnormal: Lectures at the Collège de France, 1974–75, trans. Graham Burchell, New York: Palgrave Macmillan, 2003. First published as *Les Anormaux*, Paris: Seuil/Gallimard, 1999.

The Birth of Biopolitics: Lectures at the Collège de France, 1978–79, ed. Michel Senellart, trans. Graham Burchell, New York: Palgrave Macmillan, 2008. First published as *Naissance de la biopolitique*, Paris: Seuil/Gallimard, 2004.

Dits et Écrits, Vol. 1: 1954–1975, eds. Daniel Defert and Francois Ewald, Paris: Gallimard, 1994.

Dits et Écrits, Vol. 2: 1970–1975, eds. Daniel Defert and Francois Ewald, Paris: Gallimard, 1994.

Dits et Écrits, Vol. 3: 1976–1979, eds. Daniel Defert and Francois Ewald, Paris: Gallimard, 1994.

Dits et Écrits, Vol. 4: 1980–1988, eds. Daniel Defert and Francois Ewald, Paris: Gallimard, 1994.

The Essential Works of Foucault, 1954–1984, Vol. 1: *Ethics: Subjectivity and Truth,* ed. Paul Rabinow, New York: New Press, 1998.

The Essential Works of Foucault, 1954–1984, Vol. 2: *Aesthetics, Method and Epistemology*, ed. James D. Faubion, New York: New Press, 1999.

The Essential Works of Foucault, 1954–1984, Vol. 3: *Power*, ed. James D. Faubion, trans. Robert Hurley, New York: New Press, 2001.

Foucault Live: Collected Interviews, 1961–1984, ed. Sylvère Lotringer, trans. Lysa Hochroth and John Johnston, New York: Semiotext(e), 1989.

Psychiatric Power: Lectures at the Collège de France, 1973–74, trans. Graham Burchell, New York: Palgrave Macmillan, 2006. First published as *Le Pouvoir psychiatrique*, Paris: Seuil/Gallimard, 2003.

Security, Territory and Population: Lectures at the Collège de France, 1977–78, ed. Michel Senellart, trans. Graham Burchell, New York: Palgrave Macmillan, 2009. First published as *Sécurité, territoire et population*, Paris: Seuil/Gallimard, 2004.

La Société punitive, Paris: Seuil/Gallimard, 2013.

Society Must Be Defended: Lectures at the Collège de France, 1975–76, trans. David Macey, New York: Palgrave Macmillan, 2003. First published as *Il faut défendre la société*, Paris: Seuil, Gallimard, 1997.

WORKS OF BIDET

L'État-monde, Paris: Presses Universitaires de France, 2011.

Explication et reconstruction du Capital, Paris: Presses Universitaires de France, 2004.

Exploring Marx's Capital: Philosophical, Economic and Political Dimensions, Chicago: Haymarket Books, 2009. First published as *Que faire du Capital?* Paris: Presses Universitaires de France, 1985.

'The Interpellated Subject: Beyond Althusser and Butler', in *Crisis and Critique*, vol. 2, no. 2, November, 2015.

Le Néolibéralisme, Un autre grand récit, Paris: Les Prairies Ordinaires, 2016.

Le Sujet interpellé et le corps biopolitique (in press).

Théorie de la modernité, Paris: Presses Universitaires de France, 1990.

Théorie générale, Paris: Presses Universitaires de France, 1999.

— with Gérard Démunil, *Altermarxisme* (PUF: Paris, 2007),

— edited with Stathis Kouvelakis, *Critical Companion to Contemporary Marxism*, Chicago: Haymarket Books, 2009.

INDEX

structural constraint, Foucauldian
problematic, 49
'structuralism', 123; Marxist, 16;
structural-dialectical framework,
148
'structure': inter -individual
mediation, 208; Marxist
perspective, 12, 128; meta-
Marxist' problematic, 156;
reproduction, 158–9
'struggle', from below global, 252;
war relation, 177–8
'subordination': relation of, 53;
non-reversible, 30
surplus value, 40–1, 92, 244;
accumulation of, 249; as
social power, 93; competition,
160; logic of, 195; -use-value
contradiction, 196, 211
'system', Habermasian conception
of, 179, 181
systems of difference, optimisation
of, 47

tactics, hedge funds, 251; -strategy
relation, 152, 155, 159
tasks, divsion of, 21
Taylorism, 95
teleological schema, Marx, 8
Testard, Alain, 223n
The Archaeology of Knowledge, 149
The Order of Things, 73
Therborn, Göran, 238n
Third World, 46
time: exhaustive utilisation of, 21;
harnessing of, 28; see also, space
and time
torture, spectacle of proofs of
confession, 20; Ciompi abolition
of, 107

Tosquelles, Francois, 163
Toyotism, 95
'transactional reality(ies)', 83, 86,
89, 234
'truth', 79; efficacy of, 77; Foucault
project, 73; histpry of, 74–5, 174;
notion of, 82; public character,
80

universal emancipation, project
of, 3
use-surplus values contradiction,
196, 211
USSR (Union of Soviet Socialist
Republics): as radical evil, 219;
Marxist knowledge-power
enforcement, 113; pastoral
excess, 228
utility, public, 207

Veyne, Paul, 47; 'insurrections of
conduct', 228
Vidal-Nacquet, Pierre, 162, 214
von Hayek, F., 44, 48n, 230n

wage relation, 26, 33, 99; inter-
individual, 29; labourer,
contractual freedom, 30, 191
war, 172–4; Foucault discourse,
175–6; 'of races' paradigm of,
162; 'struggle' relation, 177–8
Weber, Max, 3, 48, 218, 227
Wertkritik, 201
Williamson, Oliver, 7n
Wittgenstein, L., 75
world-system, concept of, 170, 182,
256